Old <u>KENTUCKY</u> Country

Cincinnati
Fort Thomas
Covington
Williamstown
Owenton
Carrollton
Portsmouth
Ohio Kentucky
Maysville
Vanceburg
Ohio River
Ashland
Catlettsburg
La Grange
Cynthiana
Flemingsburg
Grayson
Shelbyville
Georgetown
Carlisle
Morehead
Paris
Owingsville
Louisa
Frankfort
Versailles Lexington
Mt. Sterling
West Virginia
Winchester
Frenchburg
West Liberty
Paintsville
stown
Richmond
Irvine
Prestonsburg
ringfield
Danville
Jackson
Pikeville
Stanford
McKee
Hazard
Campbellsville
Mt. Vernon
Jenkins
Kentucky Virginia
Columbia
Somerset
London
Manchester
Whitesburg
River
Corbin
Harlan
Monticello
Pineville
kinsville
Albany
Whitley City
Middlesboro
CUMBERLAND MOUNTAIN
PINE MOUNTAIN
Kentucky
Tennessee

Scale of Miles

0   20   40   60

D. F. Archer

AMERICAN FOLKWAYS

GOLDEN GATE COUNTRY	Gertrude Atherton
WHEAT COUNTRY	William B. Bracke
SMOKY MOUNTAIN COUNTRY	North Callahan
GULF COAST COUNTRY	Hodding Carter and Anthony Ragusin
DESERT COUNTRY	Edwin Corle
BIG COUNTRY: TEXAS	Donald Day
NIAGARA COUNTRY	Lloyd Graham
DEEP DELTA COUNTRY	Harnett T. Kane
PALMETTO COUNTRY	Stetson Kennedy
NORTH STAR COUNTRY	Meridel Le Sueur
HIGH SIERRA COUNTRY	Oscar Lewis
OLD KENTUCKY COUNTRY	Clark McMeekin
LOWER PIEDMONT COUNTRY	H. C. Nixon
OZARK COUNTRY	Otto Ernest Rayburn
MORMON COUNTRY	Wallace Stegner
PITTSYLVANIA COUNTRY	George Swetnam
BLUE RIDGE COUNTRY	Jean Thomas
SHORT GRASS COUNTRY	Stanley Vestal
TOWN MEETING COUNTRY	Clarence M. Webster
ADIRONDACK COUNTRY	William Chapman White
FAR NORTH COUNTRY	Thames Williamson

Old Kentucky Country

By CLARK McMEEKIN

CLARK McMEEKIN

OLD KENTUCKY
COUNTRY

AMERICAN
FOLKWAYS

DUELL, SLOAN AND PEARCE

New York

Library of Congress Catalog Card No. 57-7574

First Edition

MANUFACTURED IN THE UNITED STATES OF AMERICA

VAN REES PRESS • NEW YORK

Contents

vii

TO ALL OTHER KENTUCKIANS, OUR KITH AND KIN.

TO THE MEN, WOMEN, AND CHILDREN WHOM WE HAVE NOT MENTIONED IN THIS BOOK.

TO THE DREAMERS AND THE DOERS, THE PLODDERS AND THE PROFLIGATES, WHO ADDED THEIR WHOLESOME SALT AND THEIR PUNGENT SPICE TO THE FEAST OF HISTORY.

Old Kentucky Country

OLD KENTUCKY COUNTRY
by CLARK McMEEKIN

Among the best novels of Kentucky in our time have been those of Clark McMeekin, and therefore it is not surprising that this new contribution to the American Folkways books by Clark McMeekin should be as readable, alive, and inviting as the best of novels.

With a love of Old Kentucky that quietly dominates every page, there goes an intimate knowledge of Kentucky's past, her flavorsome and characteristic ways, her beautiful country, her legends, her people.

The traditional Kentuckian is pictured, not as a goateed Colonel or cartoon mountaineer, but as a citizen with individuality to be found especially in the little towns:

"He may not get to the races often, but he loves and respects a fine horse to the core of his being. He is sociable, often convivial, unhurried, friendly but never 'eager,' well-mannered, a little self-important and opinionated. . . . He isn't boastful in Texas style. You see, he doesn't *think* Kentucky is the world's garden spot, God's very own country—he *knows* it."

Reading this description of Kentucky's picturesque past and of its rivers, mountains, and bluegrass country, one can appreciate how the Kentuckian feels about his land, which lies at the very heart of the republic.

This is a chronicle ranging from the exploits of Daniel Boone and George Rogers Clark and Isaac Shelby, first Governor of Kentucky, to accounts of the great Kentucky Derby and its famous horses and of the fabulous new "impounded" lakes that have come into being in recent years. Compounded of true tales and tall tales, villains and noble characters, history and folksay, OLD KENTUCKY COUNTRY offers the kind of reading that is both delightful and rewarding, a real and lasting pleasure.

CHAPTER 1

Land Where We Will Live Tomorrow

"The Sun Shines Bright"

IN THE MIDDLE of the eastern half of the United States of America, south of the beautiful meandering Ohio, west of the Big Sandy and the brooding Blue Ridge, lies Kentucky. To remove her from a relief map would give the effect of a jagged center cut chunked out of a country ham by a poor carver with a dull knife. Actually her shape suggests, rather, a whole hickory-smoked ham laid down crosswise, broadside to Virginia —ham-shaped too, by coincidence, family resemblance, and as a result of the War Between the States—Kentucky's narrow hockbone end touching the mighty Mississippi far to the west.

Old Kentucky Country lies within the confines of a state, but expands easily and often into a state of mind. "I had a Kentucky grandmother," somebody from California or Michigan will tell you, when a ship's orchestra strikes up Stephen Foster's haunting tune, "The Old Kentucky Home." "We have a picture of the old home-place. I'd like to go back there sometime. . . ."

Kentuckians anywhere, smug proprietors of the song, warm and quicken to it, too, visualizing, because of the intricate

3

divisions and startling contrasts of their native state, a wide variety of old home-places. One might see a chinked-log cabin up a Cumberland hollow, overgrown in pink-and-white calico bush and black-polished holly; another the galleried verandas, Deep South style, of a riverfront house down Hickman way in the Purchase (the hock bone). And in between, on quiet streets or shady lanes, lavishly laced with dogwood and redbud, memories would linger about many a typical L-shaped Kentucky Colonial house, made of hand-fired clay brick of a soft brown-rose color, sometimes painted white or saffron or the ubiquitous freight-train red. Occasionally these houses are tall-columned, oftener short- or not at all, but they nearly always have groves or avenues of fine old trees, beech, oak, maple, locust, elm, wild cherry, tulip poplar, ash, or walnut, and even the neglected ones have a characteristic air of dignity and tenacity.

The Rowan House at Bardstown, which inspired "The Old Kentucky Home" a hundred years ago, is a museum of unusual atmosphere. Even strangers to it have confessed an unexpected nostalgia on approaching it, and it does indeed embody romantically, and with much faithful detail, a traditional past, its day gone by "like a shadow o'er the heart."

There are plenty of other examples of a Kentuckian's old home-place. It could be of fieldstone, mortared or dry-rock, thick-walled, low-ceilinged, set close to the street for company. It could be the proverbial shack, with a hound-dog under the porch and a thorn tree or a few scrub cedars clinging to the rim of its eroded clay bank. It could be a river hovel, flooded regularly and expectedly; or a shanty boat with trotlines baited with doughballs for catfish or yellow buffalo. It might be a whitewashed tenant cottage, or an old tollgate house that once swung a revenue bar across a pike six inches deep in gray-velvet limestone dust. It could be a four-square frame with resounding porches, half-hidden by magnolia, calicanthus, and snowball bushes. But big or little, fine, poor, or middlin', it would have trees; from wind-tortured pines on a backbone ridge to giant sycamores or green willows that follow the streams, it would certainly have some kind of trees.

When the pioneers poured into Kentucke country in the last quarter of the eighteenth and the first years of the nineteenth centuries, the huge open forests offered fine homesites. Bringing what "possibles" they could, by flatboat down the Ohio, or by pack horse or hickory wagon through Cumberland Gap along the Wilderness Trail, the settlin' folks, God and the Indians willing, had come to stay, to attain the dignity of landholders, to make permanent homes.

Many were European newcomers to America—English, Scottish, Scotch-Irish, Irish, German, and French Huguenots. Others were second- and third-generation Virginians, Carolinians, Marylanders, and Pennsylvanians, who, as good farms along the seaboard became more expensive and harder to get, were enticed by the green of distant fields.

These people were not the restless wanderers, the scouts, trappers, and Long Hunters who immediately preceded them, and who shared Daniel Boone's expressed prejudice, "It crowds a man to have a cabin set up just a hundred miles from him." But they were willing to risk their lives, knowing that Indian opposition would be not only probable, but certain. Self-reliance they all had, not to say foolhardiness, for they came often in handfuls, setting up housekeeping in lonely cabins that were sometimes a week's journey from the nearest stockade.

This was a land loved and prized by powerful Indian tribes —the Cherokee, Choctaw, Creek, Wyandotte, Shawnee, and the Iroquois, chiefly—as their passageway and happy hunting ground. The translation of the name Kentucke, Kentake, Kahtentateh, or Kentateh, varies from the wistful "Land Where We Will Live Tomorrow" to the similar "Fair Land of

Tomorrow" to the grim familiar "Dark and Bloody Ground," or "River of Blood" with "Meadow" and "Prairie" somewhere in between. But regardless of its semantics, it meant so much to the Indians, who had fought over it for generations, that no "sale" to land companies or negotiated treaties of peace could be looked upon as permanent, except by the most optimistic and naïve of the pioneers.

The scouts and surveyors for the land companies—notably the Transylvania Company—had circulated tantalizing tales of the Great Meadow all along the seaboard. It was said to be fertile beyond imagination, watered by numerous navigable rivers, a network of tributary streams, and best of all by thousands of gushing springs. It was blest with salt licks, which not only supplied a crucial commodity, but attracted herds of buffalo, elk, deer. All wild game was as profuse as green leaves in summer—turkeys, grouse, quail, larks, passenger pigeons, robins, doves, and of course rabbits, squirrels, possums, and a variety of fur-bearers.

Honey would be found in this Promised Land, but most of the settlers wisely brought their milk with them, pack-train progress being necessarily slowed to the pace of the cow. Sheep and hogs were sometimes herded in by drovers, though goats would have been more practicable for homesteaders who chose the isolation of some steep Cumberland fastness. Here the hogs survived, and occasionally a few sheep, but there are known instances of generations living and dying without benefit of milk or butter, and this in a state in which dairy farming became an early important industry.

Bluegrass, Beargrass, Pennyroyal,
Purchase, and the Mountains

Kentucky's eastern mountains make up her first large natural division, the other four often being called the "Bluegrass, Beargrass, 'Pennyrile,' and Purchase." An irregular north-central circle comprises the rich rolling Bluegrass. The Beargrass is simply a name lightly given to land outside the Bluegrass. Called after Beargrass Creek in and around Louisville, it is properly a corner of the Knobs, a wide band of territory, looping irregularly around the Bluegrass, its land somewhat rougher and not quite so fertile. The Pennyroyal, named for its carpet of this sharply fragrant minty herb, takes in most of southern and western Kentucky, and tapers off to the rich cotton-growing bottomlands of the Ohio-Mississippi confluence, the Purchase, traded from the Chickasaw in 1818 by General Andrew Jackson.

Reelfoot Lake, created by the 1811 earthquake, lies largely within the Tennessee portion of the Jackson Purchase, but swampy lagoons extend into Kentucky, harboring great colonies of waterfowl, white herons, and red-winged blackbirds. Indeed, all of Kentucky's chief divisions are so interwoven, and broken again into surprise subdivisions, that a kaleidoscopic change of scene can be had by taking a short drive almost anywhere in the state.

From the most opulent fields of fine tobacco, and from lush, white-fenced pastures where the sleek thoroughbreds graze picture-book style, a ten-minute trip brings one to the rocky gorge of the Kentucky River, its gray limestone palisades unchanged since ancient-of-days. Near the eastern coalfields is a rich meadow-plateau suitably called the Little Bluegrass. The hilly western coalfield gives onto prairie-like Barrens, not barren at all, but once marked by low bush growth rather than primeval forests. Too, there are the mysterious sink strips of the Bluegrass, and the great impounded-lakes districts, the Breaks of the Sandy, the cave country with Mammoth Cave as a focal point, and the river valleys—from the Cumberland's majestic cascade to the low Thames-like banks of the Salt—and all the land is green with trees, and always has been.

In 1781, a gloomy line from a homesick letter, written by a new young citizen of Kentucke County, Virginia, to his parents in the Tidewater, notes: ". . . and I see nought much in all this big new land but trees and trees and trees to be cleared down, & my new neighbors be intemperate & full of argument . . . yet they did raise me up a rough cabin. . . ."

Early appraisals vary. "Kentucke, Elysium of supreme delight," her men "God-fearing, sober." And: "The way those Kentuckians can drink hailstorms is a caution to sinners." A neat character sketch from Collins's history is: "Look in the pockets of any Kentuckian and you are likely to find a bowie knife, a precis of a law-suit intended to defraud his neighbor of his land, a loving letter to his daughter, and a copy of 'Paradise Lost.' "

From the pen of Ann Royal, one of the earliest American women journalists, comes the pleasant: "All the Kentuckians have an artless, lofty independence in their manners, similar to the Southern people." Yet the first Bluegrass poet laureate, "The Drunken Poet of Danville," Tom Johnson, said in a book of verse, circa 1785:

> "I hate Kentucky, curse the place,
> And all her vile and miscreant race."

A little later, Hew Ainslie, the Scottish poet, grew lyrical:

> *"Gude kens I want nae better luck*
> *Than just to see ye like a buck*
> *Spanking the haughs o' auld Kentuck*
> *An' whistlin' owre the love o't."*

Theodore O'Hara, buried in Frankfort, under a monument engraved with lines from his moving poem, "The Bivouac of the Dead," was once editor of *The Frankfort Yeoman,* where some of his lighter *Kentucky Verse* appeared, his "Rollicking Rhyme" being a favorite:

> *"I'd lie for her, I'd sigh for her,*
> *I'd drink the river dry for her,*
> *But damned if I would die for her!"*

Whether he meant Kentucky or some particular Kentucky belle is uncertain. It *is* certain that plenty of men have died for Kentucky. Duncan Cassidy's *History of Lexington* says: "It was characteristic of the survivors among men who settled Kentucky, that before the Indian war whoop had ceased to echo, they set about founding . . . Transylvania, an institute of higher learning, the first one established west of the Alleghenies . . . so that Lexington came to be known as 'The Athens of the West.' "

Kentucky's story is always full of contradictions, warm hearts and hot heads, gentleness and violence, hard drinkin' and rigid teetotalism, erudition and illiteracy, outstanding statesmanship and the stuffed ballot box, the sharpest sort of horse trading and the most openhanded hospitality.

In settlin' days, the law of the land demanded that any traveler asking food and a night's lodging "be not deneyed." Now and again, one comes across an aged house cannily designed to fulfill the law and yet protect the family—an eight-room house, four up, four downstairs, with no upstairs hall or doors connecting the rooms, each of which had its own steep ladder-stairway giving only on the room below.

Today the literal Good Samaritan spirit survives almost unfailingly in the remoter hills, and without the safeguard of walled-off guest rooms. Two fishermen from Louisville, lost at night among the serpentine coves and hollows of gigantic impounded Cumberland Lake, gratefully followed a light, finding an ancient houseboat beached in a lagoon. This was the home of a small family who had made a fire on shore to fry bluegills for their supper.

"Come right up," the man-of-the-houseboat greeted them. "Set an' eat. My old woman'll stir us up some fresh pone. Stay the night. We got plenty pallet beds, plenty room."

Borderland

Perhaps the fact that the whole of Kentucky Country is a true region, shaped by quixotic natural boundaries, has much to do with her one-big-happy-wrangling-family ways. Tightly encircled by seven neighbors, she is the only state in the Union set apart from so many others, chiefly by physical barriers, her one man-made dotted line being the Tennessee border, along which the several varying local cultures meld indistinguishably. Her other three limits—the Pine Mountain Range and the big rivers—within which she has put down her roots and grafted her spreading branches, have tended at least to a degree to keep her to herself.

These same rivers did also make her accessible to the world, and she was an important goal to the very vanguard of the pioneer movement toward the "New West" in pre-Revolutionary times. They opened up her trade from Pittsburgh to New Orleans and beyond—occasional European sailing vessels

having been known to dock directly at the port of Louisville—
and have served her commercially and in a hundred other ways
ever since.

Kentucky's border rivers—the Big Sandy and Tug Fork on
the east, the Mississippi on the west, and the huge sweep of the
Ohio, her attenuated northern line—are tremendously wide,
swift streams, however, and have been effective separators. Even
today's bridges are few and far between, except in such urban
areas as Cincinnati–Covington–Fort Thomas–Newport and
Louisville–Jeffersonville–New Albany. Ferries were generally
used, and some still are, but the lack of everyday association
between the peoples of opposite shores accounts for many
noticeable differences in speech and folkways.

The major north-south cleavage was of course the natural
use of the Ohio as a long stretch of the Mason-Dixon Line.
Though Kentucky, after great agony, elected to stay in the
Union when war came, her relations with her Northern neighbors were hopelessly snarled. Mutual trade was vital, but Kentucky ports were subject to embargoes any time the government
river officials felt like clapping one on. Her goods were often
confiscated, her people swindled. On the other hand, Kentucky
had her share of war profiteers, and many a fortune was founded
on trade North or South as the opportunities came. Confederate
money was minted in Indiana and freely used on both sides of
the river until the breakdown of the Confederacy was clearly
inevitable.

On the tragic slavery question, Kentuckians again disagreed
among themselves, pro-slavery leaders inveighing against abo-
litionists and vice versa. Runaway slaves were mercilessly
hunted down and returned to their owners on the one hand,
while underground railroads zealously aided escapees on the
other. But everybody resented Northern kidnap raids in which
many Kentucky Negroes were forcibly hustled across the river,

hired out as Union Army substitutes, paid a fraction of the usual $800 bonus, their rescuers pocketing the fat remainder. General John Hunt Morgan's Ohio forays brought retaliatory shelling of Kentucky river towns, and antagonism flared along the great valley.

A valuable bone of contention to both belligerent camps, Kentucky was strongly coerced on either side. Confederate pressure, when the state tried to stay neutral, was so overriding that Union sentiment profited from it. Poor Kentucky, a house divided against herself personally rather than sectionally, brother taking up arms against brother, faced a frightful situation.

Her native son, Abraham Lincoln, later sincerely mourned and enshrined (though he polled only two votes in Lexington, his wife's home, when he was elected president), stated flatly, "If Kentucky is lost, all is lost." Another son, Jefferson Davis, also hated, loved, and memorialized, is said to have cried despairingly, "The day Kentucky failed to secede, she lost her immortal soul."

Her lifeblood was spilled on both sides, the scars of internal bitternesses healing long after the bigger issues were settled. Though she didn't leave the Union, she was still traditionally and sentimentally Southern, for her many monuments inspired by the Late Conflict—except the memorials to Lincoln—are nearly always Confederate.

Realistically, Kentucky's grass roots did not follow a Deep South pattern except in modified form. Her farms weren't the near-feudal domains of the great Southern plantations, except in a few cases. They've never been generally called plantations either, any more than ranches, but simply farms or stockfarms, but the characteristic name is places. And when they change hands, the familiar landmark names still stick to them. "That's the old McAfee place," one may be told, "across from the

Crittendens'," though nobody of either name may have lived there for years.

Traditional Kentuckians

Rich or poor, highland or lowland, typical Kentuckians share certain traits and mores. The traditional Kentuckian is, deep-down, a country boy, for Kentucky is a county state rather than a town one. "My true love, she lives in Letcher." "If Kentucky is the world's garden spot, Woodford County is the asparagus bed." People speak of visiting in Mercer, or Fayette, or Mc-Cracken, or Whitley, though the visits may include the well-known towns in these counties.

The typical Kentuckian is not the goateed colonel sipping juleps in a rocking chair. (Juleps are usually reserved for Derby guests.) Nor is he the cartoon mountaineer, lolling at the still to pick off revenuers while his wife plows. He isn't a character, though there are exceptions. But he does have individuality.

He is found in cities, in deep country, and especially in little towns—perhaps in his law office over the hardware store, or arguing politics on the courthouse steps, or driving his car leisurely down the middle of the street as his forefathers drove their horses and buggies.

Farmer or not, he is keenly aware of farm conditions and prices—especially tobacco—and he probably owns and shares out some land. He may not get to the races often, but he loves and respects a fine horse to the core of his being. He is sociable, often convivial, unhurried, friendly but never eager, well mannered, a little self-important, and opinionated.

His voice is pleasantly pitched, his r's slurred, his g's neglected as in "Mawhnin'!" Along the Tennessee-line hills he probably says "inny" instead of "any," and "nahce" for "nice." In the Bluegrass his accent is faintly marked by Virginia, but along the Ohio River and over much of the state, he is said to have a truly median speech, with only a hint of "mo' " for "more," and no trace of the north Midwest "woterrr" for "water."

This description might better be directed at a "composite" rather than at one typical Kentuckian. By majority, then, he is a Democrat and has more than likely dabbled in politics. He is a churchman, Southern Baptist, Southern Presbyterian, Southern Methodist, or Christian. He is Chesterfieldian in his relationships with his womenfolks, but expects and gets every deference and indulgence from them.

Any title, earned or complimentary, is his for life. The accusation that all Kentuckians are Colonels is an exaggeration. *Nearly* all are, thanks to obliging governors. There are books (the famous "Little Colonel" series by Annie Fellows Johnston) commemorating the traditional Kentucky Colonel through his granddaughter. There's a baseball club, too, the Louisville Colonels, and a delicious Frankfort candy, "Kentucky Colonels," to mention a few home products in the Colonel line, but many a Kentuckian also settles for Judge or Senator.

Our composite Kentuckian certainly has a nickname—Chuck or Bun or Tot or some other pet name which never takes from his dignity. "I saw Judge Puggy Smith in town. Looks a little peaked."

Passing time has broadened his views on suffrage and segregation, but not on his favorite foods. To him eating high on the hog must include "real" fried chicken, corn pudding, and old Kentucky country ham.

Closest to his heart is a fine old country ham. He certainly has never cooked one, but he knows how it's done, and gives directions in his own household and to anybody outside who will listen. Arguments rage for years over the relative merits of hams one, two, or three years old, whether they are best hickory-smoked or sugar-cured, simmered, steamed, boiled and "wrapped," or simply slowly baked. Visitors rarely escape the apocryphal story of the newcomer who threw away a superb old ham because it had tiny white spots all through it, when a ham without them would be considered scarcely fit to eat!

Our typical Kentuckian has no inferiority complex. He isn't boastful in Texas style, for example, either. Complacent he may be. You see, he doesn't *think* Kentucky is the world's garden spot, God's very own country—he *knows* it.

CHAPTER 2

This Garden Spot, Perennial Eden

"Then Dan'l Boone, from the top of an eminence with joy and wonder described the beautiful landscape of Kentucke ... the most extraordinary country on which the sun has ever shone."—John Filson, Kentucky's first historian, born 1747, killed by Indians 1788.

"Landscape of Kentucke"

THE NATIVE KENTUCKIAN of today comes naturally by his deep-seated pride in his home country, knowing how hard his forebears had to fight to get it. The Indians fended them off for just about half a century, being more jealous of intruders into their fabulous happy hunting ground than they were of invaders of their home villages. No tribe or combine of tribes had ever been able to take over Kahtentateh, and their reaction to white homesteaders was ferocious opposition, unchecked till long, long after the Revolution.

The French had forts scattered over the Indian country to the north, and there were French and Spanish strongholds down the Mississippi, but not a one in Kentucke. So it was easy for the French to inflame the Indians when they tired momentarily of scalping pioneers. It was just as easy for the British, later, to do the same thing during the Revolution. So

16

it was that, in settling the Great Meadow, more lives were lost by Indian massacre and more years consumed than in any land-snatch of comparable size in North American history.

Kentucky's topography and rich resources were gouged out and preserved in the glacial age. The imponderable ice mass crumbled at its southern edge, filling ancient rivers with stony earth. In the prehistoric deluge, melting glacial ice swelled the overwhelming rain floods so that new river channels began to be cut, the Ohio's flow was redirected, plateaux emerged, fossils were buried and preserved in shale and limestone. In R. E. Banta's interesting book, *The Ohio,* appears a full description of how the great Ohio River Valley with its feathering of tributary streams was created.

Eons after the ice had receded enough to ameliorate the frigid climate, long after the age of the huge reptiles, the first warm-blooded animals found their way into Kentucky Country. Even then the land was green, for the springs and streams abounding everywhere fed and fostered plant life. Animal life thrived for there were salt springs and licks to be found, and in northern Kentucky near the Licking River the salt deposits were accessible and enormous.

Here pools of ancient ocean silt and water had been trapped, and the blue-gray clay of the area was veined and crusted with salt, so necessary to mammal life. In pioneer days and for some time afterward the "mining" or refining of salt was a considerable industry, the mineral being so plentiful that many a stockade had its own salt spring as well as its more important fresh-water one.

Graveyard of the Mammoths

Big Bone Lick, one of the famous landmarks of discovery days, was a hunter's dream-come-true, for here the herds of buffalo and deer came constantly to lick the salt they had to have. Dramatic evidence of the nightmarish earlier animal life here was found in the Graveyard of the Mammoths close by. On acres and acres of bare clay, sunk and flattened as if by the palms of gargantuan hands, were laid out the huge skeletons and skulls of prehistoric visitors here—the great sloth, the giant elk, the arctic elephant, the mastodon maximus, the hairy mammoth, and other animals long extinct.

Drawn to the great licks less by such curiosities than by the fine buffalo hunting, and the salt deposits there, the first white hunters paid little attention to these secrets of the past. They were conscious of special Indian danger here, as they were at any of the salt licks. Daniel Boone himself was captured once at the Lower Blue Licks, where he was busily boiling off salt. Many ambush attacks were made on "salt parties," and the disastrous Battle of the Blue Licks in 1782 brought death or capture to some seventy Kentuckians.

The story of the first human life in the Kentucky region is also associated with the many salt licks, for it was near one of them that the earliest human remains have been found. These aborigines probably came here about 5000 B.C., and we are told that they may have feasted on some of the very animals whose immense bones formed part of the Graveyard of the Mammoths. Since the first human beings have left us nothing to indicate that they lived in groups, we can only imagine their foraging here in indescribable fear and loneliness.

Even so, the discovery of salt in abundance was probably as important to them as it was to the animals. Here the first inhabitants of Kentateh set up housekeeping in convenient caves. With only sticks and stones for weapons, if they did succeed in preying on the mammoths, one wonders how on earth they could have managed to kill them, for they have left to us only scorched bits of stone, along with a few identifiable splinters of their own puny bones, to attest their crude and bare existence. A natural guess would be that they endured a great many meatless days until convenient mortal duels between big animals flooded the markets for the hungry human population.

Since the dim derivative day of the cave man, several tribes and cultures have flowered and faded in Kentucky. Some of these have left distinct records of their ways of life and their accomplishments, others merely a few relics which have allowed antiquarians to piece out frail but logical sketches of their customs. There have also been imagination-catching legends handed down in the savage tribes who met the first of the white pioneers—stories of pale Indians said to be descended from the lost Welsh explorer Madoc; a race of blond giants long thought to have been of Viking extraction; a mysterious indigenous extinct tribe skilled in arts, medicine, and precious-metal work.

Actually there isn't enough evidence to support any of these romantic stories of vanished civilizations, the only proof-positive left to us being that of the existence of American Indian tribes here. But so widespread were the legends and so surprising in nature that one still wonders, and even hopes that some unexplored cave may someday be found with answers to these tantalizing questions.

Caves Are Convenient

All over Kentucky Country there were plenty of caves for the wandering savage to make use of, not only in the honey-combed Mammoth Cave area in the mid-southwest, but along the rivers, in the mountains, in the Knobs, and scattered over the Bluegrass. For thousands of years primitive man had no housing problem here, but his isolated approach to civilization was slow and fumbling.

Much use of the caves has been made in our present-day state of enlightenment. One has only to drive through the country, nearly anywhere on a winding road, to see written in wavering whitewashed letters on the face of some lovely vine-draped rock cliff: "Daniel Boone's Cave, Hot Dogs and Soft Drinks," or "Jesse James' Hideout—*Eats*," or "Pioneer Trail Grotto—Cold Beer to Go," "Cave-in Lunch," or "Cavern-Tavern."

More attractive use of the scattered little caves has been made by Kentucky children over the years. To wade in icy water or play hide-and-seek, just stretching the bounds of safety a little, to enjoy the sense of mystery and danger of a few steps down a black passageway, to imagine eyes glowing in the dark, to feel the brush of a bat's wing and run, run, *run* for the beautiful ragged light of the entrance, can pale any cheek of tan.

Supplies, treasures, even livestock were hidden in the caves during the Civil War. And from the earliest food-safe to the very reign of the electric refrigerator, the little caves have served as cool-storage rooms, their springs as iceboxes. Often one wall of the many little springhouses found all over the state is a natural rock face, the other three being thick fieldstone, with a mossy shingle roof. Sometimes only the opening of a little cave spring is roofed over to shelter the milk crocks cooling in the cold clear water.

Centuries after the era of the nomad cave man in Kentucky came the Indian Knoll culture, widespread over the Mississippi Valley. The peoples of this persuasion evidently specialized in shore dinners, for the knolls for which their civilization was later named were simply huge stacks of mussel shells. The streams in those days were full of a variety of shellfish, and either by chance or because they felt the knolls to be of some decorative or protective value, Kentucky's first villagers accumulated tons on tons of shells.

The discovery of these knolls led to the finding of skeletons and artifacts of bone, clay, and of course shell, and to the tracing of laid-out villages or communities. There was evidence that huts of brush and rock were used as shelters, quite a step from cave life.

The Mound Builders who came much later—they first lived in Kentucky about a thousand years ago—left burial mounds, temples, cities, and military escarpments in many places in the Ohio Valley. An advanced people, they farmed corn and plowed with sharp stones. Some of their jewelry and tools, their pipes and shards and weapons, can be seen in museums, well-made articles of stone and wood with some copper.

The building of these very first mounds was certainly a group project and a backbreaking one. Without horses or any kind of beasts of burden, wheel, or lever, the earth had to be carried by crude drags or possibly baskets. Some of the mounds have a base diameter of more than two hundred feet, and after centuries of packing and eroding are still fifty or more feet high. These weren't the hit-or-miss shell knolls of dim prehistory, but the result of community planning beyond the range of any other primitive Kentuckians of the period.

Mound Builders and Empire Builders

In the fifteen- and sixteen-hundreds, a strikingly advanced race or tribe of Mound Builders lived in parts of Kentucky and in other spots along the lower Ohio Valley. A part of the so-called Middle Mississippi culture, these were said to be a friendly and startlingly civilized strain. The artifacts they have left to us—and it is a pity that so many of their burial mounds were despoiled by gold diggers and curio hunters before anything was done to protect them or supervise their opening—are impressive. Much of their pottery has been saved, some of excel·lent quality and beautifully decorated. Their tools, spears, bows, and arrows were of superior workmanship, too; and they farmed corn and tobacco and squash, beans, and several root vegetables. Some of their elaborate fortifications have been preserved and restored, but perhaps their most remarkable legacy is their etchings, portraits and designs delicately cut on slate, wood, sandstone, and mother-of-pearl.

In the seventeenth century, marauding bands of French and Spanish empire builders exterminated the Mound Builders, except for the few who escaped and joined the Cherokee, Chickasaw, Shawnee, Iroquois, and other tribes wandering the glades of Kentucke.

Sometimes the white explorers were in turn killed or "captivated" by Indians, sometimes they were well received. There is a record of a Dutchman, Arnout Viele, from Pennsylvania, who paddled down the Ohio from the Allegheny in 1692. He and his party of whites and Indians visited a Shawnee camp at the Mississippi confluence for a couple of years of fur trading and apparently happy comradeship.

With the exceptions of a few such camp-villages, the tribes, however powerful, didn't live in the Great Meadow, but used it as a hunting ground, the deer and buffalo roaming and ranging predictably around the salt licks, the deep forests offering small game aplenty, the network of streams abounding in fish. The country was open and ideal as a passage-through from and to any direction, yet the cane brakes, great trees, and shelves of rock provided cover. Wild fruits, pawpaws, grapes, berries, and nuts were profuse; the climate was temperate; the waterways, superhighways of the period, were extremely convenient for pirogue or war canoe, and were dependable guides to anyone "momentarily bewildered."

There is no certainty as to the identity of the first white man to view any part of Kentucky Country. Rafinesque, self-styled "odd fish," writer, professor at Transylvania, botanist of the early 1800's, states the "fact" that Hernando De Soto or his successor Moscoso actually saw the western fringe of what is now Kentucky about 1540, but no authority for such a declaration was given.

Among the famous French to lay eyes on the land—the same western portion—were Father Jacques Marquette, Louis Joliet, and René Robert Cavelier, Sieur de La Salle. It has been variously recorded that La Salle with a party of Frenchmen left the Illinois River in 1682, cruising down the Mississippi to the Delta, claiming possession of lands east and west in the name of King Louis the Great. The group stopped to trade with Indians at a point which, from its description, was thought to be the mouth of the Ohio. A year or so later, La Salle's party "placed themselves under the protection of the British and sold the latter a vast tract" which included Kentucky.

This rather strange deal took place in Albany, New York, in 1684. La Salle is said to have surrendered then a "deed of sale" to Governor Howard of Virginia and Colonel Dungan of New York during a treaty with the Five Nations. The Crown of England, in chartering the colony of Virginia under Captain

John Smith in 1607, had included the land of Kentucke, the English claim to the immense combined freehold resting on Sir Walter Raleigh's discovery of the (present) North Carolina shores in 1584, a century before La Salle's Mississippi trip, but apparently didn't object to buying it now.

Kentucke had no colonial or county status, and its extent and possibilities were largely anybody's guess. English scouts had reached the Ohio shores in 1671, but the intense hardships and Indian hostility discouraged any idea of trying to settle the land. Virginia wanted to keep possession, but was unsure she did possess the Great Meadow and was entirely too busy with her own problems to bother with new ones, however fertile the fields. Even the conjecture by some explorers that the "New River" might lead to a western sea or a southern one and thence to the Orient didn't fire British or Colonial zeal to take decisive action in establishing ownership.

Then in the early 1700's French activity began to cause concern. Though the English colonies insisted that any French claim based on La Salle's expedition or anybody else's was absurd, they realized late in the day that French trading posts and forts, scattered from Canada to the Delta, were acts of possession and very real threats. French-Indian alliances also were viewed with alarm, and determination to have and hold the heart of the continent firmed up as the second half of the eighteenth century began. Land companies sprang up, eager pioneers studied widely deviating maps and screwed up courage to consider floating down the perilous Ohio by flatboat or trekking the mountain trails and Cave Gap through the Cumberlands to gain rich holdings, not merely as a spine-tingling dream, but as a probability.

Dr. Thomas Walker went through Cave Gap—changing its name to Cumberland Gap—in 1750, reporting that he had "read many signs on tree and rock of white men's journeying north and west," though he himself went no farther than the far eastern sections of Kentucke. The Long Hunters, some forty strong, went from the Yadkin Valley far deeper into the wilderness, staying so long (months for some, years for others) that they earned their half-envious, half-reproachful nickname. Wanderers by preference, most of them, of shy and lonely habit, they learned woodcraft and Indian lore considerably beyond distinguishing between the true or false cry of owl or whippoorwill, or the innocent or ominous snapping of the proverbial twig.

Christopher Gist, also from the Carolina Yadkin neighborhood, made an Ohio Valley trip as an agent for the Ohio Land Company, in 1751, repeating it in 1753, guiding the young George Washington (barely "of age") who had been sent by Governor Dinwiddie of Virginia to try to treat with the French and Indians. The French officers pooh-poohed the idea that England held any claim to the New West, and together with their Indian allies began the French and Indian Wars which were to harass the colonies for nine bitter years.

Though the Treaty of Paris in 1763 marked France's final defeat and gave England nearly all of the coveted New West, the Indians had no idea of letting white settlers ruin their hunting ground, or take over any part of the Ohio Valley—treaties to the contrary—if they could help it. Intentions were made fully clear by their hunting down and killing all the wandering whites they could find, or on occasion—as in the case of that extraordinary scout Daniel Boone, when he was picked up by a scalping party in 1769, on his first penetration into the very valley of the Kentucky River—letting one off with stern direction to go home and tell his adventure-honing friends that "the wasps and yellow-jackets" were waiting in ambush for them.

Though members of their party were killed, Boone and his

brother Squire stayed on in the wilderness for two years, "hunting with plentiful abandon while discovering natural wonders to delight a man's soul as in a paradise."

Here was quite a kettle of fish. The colony of Virginia had full legal right to a tremendous orchard of forbidden fruit. A new "hatch" of land companies sold claims. For months and years, pioneers gathered in the Watauga Valley, eager to press on into Eden. Up at Redstone Old Fort (Brownsville) in Pennsylvania, settlers' flatboats were being built and floated on the Monongahela to Pittsburgh for the hazardous downstream journey into new homelands, possibly but not very probably on the Kentucke shores.

The first two concerted and notable attempts to found permanent Kentucky settlements—the route of one party being the Ohio and Kentucky Rivers, the other overland through Cumberland Gap—ended in tragedy. Boone, after many trips on his own, led a group of about a dozen families, including his own, along the mountain trails to Kentucky, but at the Gap watchful Indians set upon them, killing Boone's first-born son and five other men. Boone would have continued the journey, but his cohorts refused.

In that same year, 1773, thirty-two determined men, going by river with James Harrod, established Harrodsburg (Harrodstown, then, in the southern part of the Bluegrass, very near the Kentucky and Dick's Rivers), the first-to-be-permanent settlement. But this venture, along with plans for a network of towns and nearby stations, was abandoned for the time, after members of the party were killed and wounded in Indian attack.

In spite of this ever-present danger, surveying parties and single and collective scouts and agents continued to spy out the land, among them the colorful Simon Kenton who "ran the gantlet eight times," John Findley, James McBride, Thomas

Bullitt, the McAfee brothers, and many others. But no other single woodsman can be credited with such astonishing achievements as those of Daniel Boone in bringing permanent settlers into Kentucke, blazing most of the Wilderness Trail, leading pioneer wagon trains even as he created the road, trees being cut down under his direction by woodsmen, the families following and never being out of earshot of the ringing axes ahead.

Captured again and again, he made friends with the Indians, maneuvered himself out of the most hair-trigger situations, escaped repeatedly, warned, protected, and encouraged the pioneer stockades, yet dealt with an almost unique fairness with his "friends and blood brothers" in the Indian nations.

A brave and simple man—"I am no smooth hero, do not make me one, but a rugged man who loved the sun." (from *The Bronze Hunter*)—Boone has inspired many a statue, portrait, book, and poem.

Lord Byron's *Don Juan* contains an oversimplified tribute:

> *"Of all men saving Sylla the man-slayer,*
> *Who passes for in life and death most lucky,*
> *Of the great names which in our faces stare,*
> *The General Boon, back woodsman of Kentucky*
> *Was happiest among mortals anywhere;*
> *For killing nothing but a bear or buck, he*
> *Enjoy'd the lonely, vigorous, harmless days*
> *Of his old age in wilds of deepest maze."*

To any native Kentuckian Boone is far, far more than that. Among those very first, whose bare, moccasined, or booted feet stepped off the beaten paths, or drifted down strange new waterways, fully aware that there was no likely return to past home or familiar comfort, he was pre-eminent. Though he was defrauded of his own original claims by legal technicality, and though he suffered loss of dear ones and the lesser disappointments of being robbed of pelts and furs trapped at the cost of keen privation, his philosophy was always one of brotherly love and mature acceptance.

Go to the graves of Daniel Boone and his wife Rebecca. Side by side they lie on a high promontory overlooking the winding green Kentucky River and the beautiful little city of Frankfort far below. The river travels now as it did then through rich and gracious meadowlands, past gray rock palisade and noble forest. Lay your living hands on the two mounds so close together and know that beneath this very earth is dust once sentient as your own fingertips. Kentucky was to them indeed "Fair Land of Tomorrow," "The Coming Day." Their footprints laid a light but lasting pattern in this soil, and in their tomorrow they have given us our yesterday.

CHAPTER 3

Big Bones and Stout Hearts

"Despite the Danger"

YESTERDAY is regarded by today's native Kentuckian in a very personal way. The Lares and Penates of Kentucky Country have enough age on them—about one hundred and eighty years —for deep-rooted family trees, but not too much for "memory-to-memory" communication.

Much of Kentucky's story has been personal, for the land was first invaded by scattered single spies and not battalions. No enormous battles have been fought on her soil, but one translation of her name—The Dark and Bloody Ground—has been borne out in thousands of isolated individual cases. Every family treasures handed-down stories of Great-grandfather's bravery or old Aunt Fronnie's outwitting of the red varmints, passed on from generation to generation, and happily set down, now and then, in diary or journal.

Almost any old house has its collection of Indian stone weapons picked up on the place—from delicate, tiny arrowheads, exquisitely carved and needle-sharp for shooting birds, to heavy smooth-worn war clubs. Such relics are still found occasionally, attesting the great number of Indians who once enjoyed our groves. Unfortunately for them, the pioneers wanted this land, too.

Neither the white settlers nor the Indians barred any holds in their bitter struggle to keep the beloved country. There were hundreds of cases where a small pioneer family would be set upon and destroyed, the baby's brains dashed out, while murder and captivation complete with torture and running of the gantlet were meted out to the parents and older children. Unjust retaliation followed, as in the case of the wise and superior Mingo Chief Logan, Boone's friend, who returned from dealing fairly and even generously with the whites to find his lodge burned and his entire family cruelly slain by reckless white killers.

Of course no Kentuckian today is descended from pioneers who dealt with Indians in any way other than bravely and fairly! Such incidents as sharp sales, the murder of hostages, mass exiles, the enforcing of treaties designed to cheat and exploit to conspicuous excess, were rationalized by calling attention to Indian atrocities and double dealings. The dumping of a few wagonloads of poisoned cabbages at the outskirts of Louisville in the late eighteenth century—an occurrence for which nobody could ever be found who was responsible, who had had a hand in it, or who even had the slightest knowledge of it—solved one of the many Indian problems, petty thievery.

Twinges of conscience were occasionally expressed for the seizing of the happy hunting ground, some of them taking bizarre forms. In the middle 1800's, for example, large groups of the Cherokee, long exiled to Oklahoma, were brought back at considerable public and private expense to be educated at a boarding school near Georgetown, a charming old small town in a good Baptist neighborhood in the Bluegrass.

The Indians didn't like the well-intentioned strict regime of boarding school, and the venture lasted only a short time. The white friends of the students were interested in the Western ponies the Indians had used for the long journey from "the Territory," however, and found it easy to trade them out of them. So the upshot of the proceeding was that the Indians walked home, and a fine infusion of toughness and stamina was added to the blood lines of certain trotting strains and pacers. Thus all onus to do right by the ousted redman was dissolved, and today not even an acre of Indian reservation exists in his beloved "Fair Land of Tomorrow," the only town bearing an Indian name being Paducah.

It is true that "Cherokee Indians in full war-paint, armed with bows, arrows, and blow-guns, will invade their historic hunting ground here tomorrow for their annual two-day conquest," to quote the *Louisville Courier-Journal* of October 18, 1956. This is in celebration of the Daniel Boone Festival held each fall at Barbourville, with such special features as Indian feasts, pageants, and the signing of the Cane Treaty which gives the Cherokee who live in North Carolina's Quallah Reservation the right to come over into Kentucky to cut all the cane they want from the brakes of Knox County.

A high point of the 1956 festival was a visit of Oklahoma Cherokee, whose ancestors were banished by President Andrew Jackson from their homes in North Carolina, Georgia, and Tennessee to the old Indian Territory. This reunion, about a hundred and thirty years afterward, was enlivened by archery contests, blow-gun demonstrations, hog-calling, speechmaking, and powwows. The Cherokee from the Smoky Mountains, regular attendants at the Barbourville Festival, are intimate friends of the townspeople on first-names terms, and together do honor to the memory of Dan'l Boone. Back in the 1770's, opinion was more partisan.

The distinguished Kentucky historian, Lewis Collins, makes it very clear that our first pioneers, for a while at least, outdid the savages at "playing Indian." To wit: "The world has scarcely presented so thorough a condition of personal freedom as that enjoyed by the pioneer hunters of Kentucky. Art could make no palace so grand as their home. . . . Wherever the pioneer went his hands obtained him all that was necessary to his existence. The forest furnished him more than he could eat. . . . The skins that enwrapped his food became his own clothing. The canopy of heaven was his roof, the ground that brought forth so abundantly if he chose to till it, was his bed. . . . If the land were not his own he made it so by clearing a spot and carving his name on a tree as record of ownership; he planted a few seed and went away; he returned and gathered his crops. His life was one of constant danger but scarcely one of toil—one of ever-fresh excitement that he loved despite the danger."

In the diary of a pioneer of 1775, an amusing line is: "No scalding of bedsteads, sweeping of yards or scouring of floors here!"

So from the beginning we see the Kentucky settler as easy-going, individual, robust, independent, reckless, self-sufficient, never quite believing that the torch or tomahawk that wiped out his neighbor's family and worldly goods would ever catch him unawares.

Soon after his attractive picture of pioneer freedom, Historian Collins makes lyrical comment on pioneer health. "Physical nature had no real want which the forest did not supply. The purest air of heaven combined with the high exercise of the chase to produce the most perfect bodily health. Sickness was the greatest stranger in early Kentucky. Death from natural causes was so remarkable that on one occasion when a young man was taken sick and died after the usual manner of nature, the women of the fort sat up all night gazing upon him as an object of beauty."

Violent death was of course a constant hazard, yet few pioneers lived in a stockade any longer than was considered absolutely necessary—and sometimes not that long, or even at all! This may account for the remarkable freedom from epidemics—typhoid, smallpox, the plague—which later beset the growing towns. The crowded, unsanitary conditions in a stockade—a handful of blockhouses in a quadrangle made of solid walls of skinned trees, where the water was threatened by almost nonexistent sewer arrangements, where livestock and people were jam-packed—were probably more uncomfortable to the hardy settlers than outside uneasiness about "Injuns," though this viewpoint seems foolhardy when we read of even a few fears-come-true.

Dark and Bloody Ground

As eager as the pioneers—both men and women—were, to come into the New West, the first white woman known to have set foot in Kentucke country came most unwillingly. She was brought here as an Indian captive, adopted by the Shawnee.

Mary Draper Ingles, mother of two little children, with a baby on the way, was abducted from her home in the small settlement of Draper's Meadows, Virginia, at the head of the Roanoke River, in 1755. After six months' march, the Shawnee war party reached their town on the Scioto River in southern Ohio, where they met in council to decide the fate of their prisoners—Mary Ingles, her three children (her baby having been born on the march), and her sister, Elizabeth. Elizabeth was forced to run the gantlet. Christopher Gist, famous agent for the Ohio Company, was visiting the town, and wrote an account of the scene:

"Her eyes blazed defiance on the murderous rabble. At the

word of the chief she sprang forward between the lines and was
assailed by the merciless mob. She fought fiercely. She snatched
weapons, over-threw warriors, beat down squaws, brushed aside
youths and dogs. How she reached the council house she never
remembered . . . suffering from many wounds and her arm
again broken. . . ."

Mary's punishment was more subtle. Her children were
taken from her and sent to separate towns, the younger two soon
dying. But Mary herself, a favorite of the chief, was adopted as
his daughter and worked with the squaws, often fishing and
foraging with them on the Kentucky side of the Ohio River.
Her chance to escape came in the fall of 1756, after she had
made a long red shirt of cloth bartered from French traders, the
stylish garment so pleasing the chief that he paraded the streets
in it by the hour.

The chief now insisted that Mary accompany him everywhere
he went, and on a salt-making expedition into Kentucky, when
camp had been pitched at Big Bone Lick in northern Kentucky,
she managed to get away. An old Dutch woman, also a captive,
casually walked off with Mary "to gather fox grapes" while the
Indians were boiling down the several hundred gallons of
saline water for the resulting bushel of salt. After months of
extreme hardship, hiding from pursuers, living on nuts and
berries, the two women made their way along rivers and over
mountains back to Draper's Meadows and Mary's husband,
William Ingles.

After years of effort to ransom Elizabeth and Mary's son
Tommy, success came, though Tommy, like many other young
captives, was now thoroughly Indian in speech and habit and
"carried an Injun look to him all his days."

Besides being a tale of remarkable fortitude and bravery,
the saga of Mary Ingles had much practical value to surveyors
and scouts setting out for various spots in Kentucke. Her

description of the Shawnee towns, her estimation of their strength, her knowledge of Indian habits, travel routes, and campsites, of the streams, springs, salt licks, and general features of the wild region in which she had managed to survive, were helpful to more than a few of the explorers of the day.

Especially amazing to her listeners was the ancient wonder of Big Bone Lick, some ten acres of packed clay strewn with mastodon and mammoth skulls massive as beech trunks, two feet wide between eye sockets which were often eighteen inches in diameter. There were teeth seven inches by five and weighing some ten pounds each, tusks eleven feet long, thighs four feet long, ribs five or six feet long and useful as tentpoles!

Occasional scouts had brought back tales of the macabre scene in the early 1700's. John Sallings of Williamsburg, Virginia, who claimed he visited the place in 1730, and a French Canadian named Longueil, who saw it in 1739, are thought to have been the first white men there, but about Mary Ingles's being the first woman there is very little question.

The big bones became in demand as curios as pioneering increased, and brisk trading and "ordering" went on. Tons of relics were carried away, and tons and tons more were dug up. In 1803, Dr. Goforth gave a collection to an English traveler, one Thomas Ashe, to be exhibited in Europe. Ashe sold them, instead, and pocketed the money, but specimens were later shipped to the Royal College of Surgeons in London, and to Dublin and Edinburgh. In 1805, Thomas Jefferson gave some to the American Philosophical Society and to a French naturalist. It therefore took little more than fifty years to scatter the relics of these creatures, at least some of whom predated mankind in the Dark and Bloody Ground.

How It Feels to Be Scalped

There were many instances of children, such as Tommy Ingles, being kidnaped and adopted into savage tribes. Often these children, after years of living as Indians, refused to return to their own families when the opportunity came, or if they did return found it a strange and difficult life. Such a case was that of young Tom Chenoweth. At fourteen he was captured while carrying grist to the mill, and he was returned to his family after six years of Indian life. His return is said to have amounted almost to a second captivity, since he came with great reluctance, having lost all taste for the ways of civilization, preferring buckskins to homespun, sleeping on the floor feet toward the fire or rolled in a blanket on the ground outside, a true story which would certainly have great appeal to present-day Davy Crocketts, but must have been painful for young Tom and all his family, until he became adjusted.

The Chenoweths, whose descendants are present-day citizens of Jefferson County, were from the beginning prominent in and around Louisville, part and parcel of the rewards and hardships of pioneering. Richard and Margaret, with their two sons and two daughters, came from Berkeley County, Virginia, down the Ohio by flatboat with the party of Lieutenant Colonel George Rogers Clark to Corn Island, forerunner of the village of Louisville. A carpenter and builder, Richard Chenoweth, at Clark's request, directed and helped to erect the Fort-on-Shore. Two cannons were left to protect it when the military expedition pushed on northwest.

As soon as possible, Chenoweth and the hardier souls pulled away from the main group to form settlements on Beargrass Creek and other nearby likely spots. The Chenoweth place, some fifteen miles east of Louisville near Middletown, soon boasted a good double cabin of puncheon logs for the family, sturdy outbuildings for their slaves, barns for stock, and a fortified springhouse to be used in case of Indian attack.

After two years of peace and prosperity the dreaded attacks did come. First their horses were stolen; and when the "men" went out to search for them, they were ambushed by Indians, ten-year-old James being struck in the hip by an arrow which he managed to pull out, though the tip broke off and had to be "gashed out" by a doctor years later. It was during the following summer that the older brother Tom was carried into captivity, and then in 1789 when the family sat at the supper table one evening the Indians attacked once more.

Young James was struck on the head with a tomahawk, but managed to crawl outside and hide in a heap of firewood where he lost consciousness. Coming to, later, hearing no sound, he was sure his family had all been killed or captured, so he crawled into the woods. Here his faithful dog found him, licked the blood from his face, and here the two were found in the morning by a neighbor who organized a party to return to the ruined Chenoweth house. The house had been fired but hadn't burned down, and inside they found six-year-old Naomi, the youngest child, safe in a roll of bedding where she had been overlooked by the war party. The other members of the family had been wounded but had escaped to neighbors' houses, except for Mrs. Chenoweth who was discovered in the springhouse.

She had been scalped and left for dead, but she was still alive and when her strength returned was able to describe her scalping. A whooping Indian, she said, wound her long hair about his hand to get good purchase, then "with the dullest and jaggedest knife I ever felt" cut all around "just below the hair line," then, with his knife held between his teeth, he wrapped both hands in her hair, set his foot against her back, and tore off her scalp, exposing her bare skull. Somehow, after he had gone, she managed to creep to the springhouse but couldn't walk the plank leading to the loft and possible safety, though she could see it clearly in the light of the fires the Indians were setting to burn her house. Remembering a hymn, "Jesus Can Make My Path to Shine," she told her family later, she rose and "as an act of faith, like Peter walking on the water," she took the few steps "and walked the plank unto salvation." Her hair never grew again, and she wore a mob cap for the rest of her long and noble life.

This touching and bone-chilling story was published in 1921 by Alfred Pirtle, a great-nephew of James Chenoweth, and is a dramatic example of Kentucky family sagas handed down in diary and journal, a valuable heritage to later generations.

From such sources we have the story of the Linn boys, and three friends, the eldest in the group thirteen, youngest nine, going duck hunting in Louisville's early days. The Linns needed meat for family food, their father having been killed by Indians and the two lads left as providers for their mother. When they were all picked up by Indians and marched off, the older boys, who could "make use of a gun and were therefore ranked as fort-men," and even the nine-year-old, fully realized that a moment's hesitation or complaint would mean instant death, so they "kept up the cruel pace by the hardest."

Arriving dead-beat at the Indian encampment, the boys were pelted by the squaws and their children with sticks and stones, the traditional welcome to captives. Giving a good account of themselves in the free-for-all that followed, they were initiated into a new life, fitting into it so well that they soon became trusties and were allowed to go fishing, guarded only by an aged warrior and squaw. Determined to escape, the five youngsters unhesitatingly killed the two old Indians, without helpful hints from comic book or television as to how to go about it.

For weeks they wandered in the woods, knowing they were being hunted, dodging their trackers, living on roots and berries, taking bearings from sun and stars. Reaching the Indian shore of the Ohio, they made their way to a point opposite Louisville. They could see their friends and neighbors moving about, but all their shouting and hand-waving had no effect, for the townspeople were accustomed to Indian decoys and wary of them. The desperate children had to make a rude raft of willow saplings and vines with which to brave the river, which was over a mile wide and full of whirlpools, the current, sweeping toward the falls and the horseshoe bend below, being extremely strong and swift. Even with the raft it was a remarkable enough crossing, and then at mid-channel the boys looked back to see pursuers on the shore shooting at them. But make it they did, our young heroes whose training had been grimly realistic enough to save them.

Kentucky's First Abe Lincoln

Naturally Kentucky is proud of such records, thankful that so many have been saved, for now and then, even today, new ones come to light. A recent find was made in Bardstown, an original Catholic colony settled in 1785 largely by migrating Marylanders, a beautiful old town famed for delightful old houses and a variety of other distinctions, such as Kentucky's first (except for Dr. Thomas Walker) practicing physician, Dr. Hart; Salem Academy, an early school of high standard; historic St. Joseph Pro-Cathedral, Nazareth Convent, and the Trappist monastery of Gethsemani; early resident John Fitch, inventor of one of the first steamboats; and Talbott Inn, a fine example of the old post tavern.

This newest find was made by women of a national historical

society who were delving through dusty boxes in the old Nelson County courthouse, which fortunately had never been damaged by fire or flood or cleaned up by Philistines. All of the valuable material found was microfilmed and presented to colleges, libraries, and clubs for accessibility to students. Among items of interest were a letter about a land suit, from George Mason, author of the Virginia bill of rights; papers concerning John Fitch, steamboat inventor; marriage bonds from 1784-1838; dancing-school subscription lists of both Louisville and Bardstown, 1794; stampless letters from 1784-89; twenty-four original commissions for sheriffs and justices of the peace signed by early Virginia and Kentucky governors; land warrants on sheepskin signed by Governor Henry Lee of Virginia and by Isaac Shelby, Kentucky's first governor. On one warrant, William Henry Harrison, governor of Indiana Territory, had signed his name and affixed a seal of a running buffalo; and Patrick Henry's characteristic signature appeared on six writings.

But perhaps the most widely interesting discovery was the recorded death date of Abraham Lincoln's grandfather, along with other data about him to support and amplify the findings of Lincoln genealogists and researchers. In a pile marked "Promiscuous Papers" was considerable evidence of the elder Abraham's circumstances. Having been a captain of militia in the Shenandoah Valley, and having served there as a judge advocate for a time, he was also a man of property. His treasury warrant for land in Kentucky, entitling him to 2,268½ acres, a very sizable tract even in those days, amounted to a payment of about nine thousand dollars.

It seems that he offered to give a thousand acres to a man by the name of Reid (or Reed) and that a lawsuit concerning the matter developed years later. The whys and wherefores of all this would be a particular problem in detection for the Lincoln scholar. Perhaps some private trade or "understanding" existed between the two men, which led afterward to misunderstanding.

In any event, the pioneer Abraham Lincoln, related to Daniel Boone by blood, friendship, and point of view, believed in the bright future of Kentucke enough to go there in 1780, enter a holding of four hundred acres in Jefferson County near Long Run and another of eight hundred below the Green River. He then returned to Virginia to finish the winding up of his affairs and prepare to bring his family to the new land.

Ida Tarbell in her distinguished book, *In the Footsteps of the Lincolns,* mentions that the scholarly Reverend Lewis A. Warren speaks of finding evidence of Lincoln's purchase of the two-thousand-acre tract. Perhaps the prospect of clearing such a monstrous slice of wilderness singlehanded was too awesome even for the ambitious young Lincoln. Perhaps he bought it chiefly for investment value for the future. Or possibly it was too far from the protection of a stockade to offer any hope of safety.

In 1782, Kentucky's "Year of Blood," the Lincoln family made their daring move west—Abraham, his wife Bathsheba, their four children. Mordecai the eldest was about ten years old; Thomas, future father of the sixteenth president of the United States, was four. The four-hundred-acre tract on Long Run was their destination, and here for four busy, hopeful years the young father worked hard to clear his land and establish a cabin home for his family.

The Filson Club of Louisville, named for Kentucky's first historian, has made scholarly and rewarding efforts over the years to reconstruct as many details of the Lincolns' early period here as possible—the location and precise survey of their land, the listing of their possessions, their first dwelling place, and so on. These painstaking investigators unearthed the remnants of a blockhouse and its enclosure some time ago, that they—as well as Miss Tarbell and several other fine researchers—believe to be those of the old Hughes Station stockade. It is very near the first Lincoln farm and must have been the family headquarters.

Knowing only too well the threat of Indians on the prowl, Abraham Lincoln, like other pioneer farmers, felt compelled to dare the danger over and over again. The land *had* to be cleared, crops *must* be planted to provide the family support. The touching picture of the determined young farmer working hard while his children played or stood guard was an accepted part of daily life, and on May 17, 1786, he took eight-year-old Thomas to help him work and Mordecai, fourteen, to mount guard, gun in hands.

When an Indian materialized from the brush, shooting and killing Abraham at his plow, and snatching up little Thomas, Mordecai, too late to save his father, was able to bring down the Indian and rescue his younger brother from captivity and probable death. So it was that in spite of the tragedy to the family, Thomas was saved to play his part as a vital link in American history, for in time his son Abraham was to be accounted great, not only in his own age and country, but for all ages to come, throughout our world.

CHAPTER 4

Howling Wilderness and Fruitful Field

Sold for Ten Thousand Pounds

THE FIRST "permanent wave" of settlers broke over Kentucky Country in 1775. They came in pack trains, with an occasional wagon, driving a few farm animals, bringing a handful of "pots, pans and necessaries." Several families would band together, engage a scout, and start out. As in any frontier movement, there were land companies busily acquiring claims and grants to parcel out and sell sight-unseen, but most of the early comers preferred to stake their own claims and make possession its proverbial nine points of the law.

The Transylvania Company, headed by Colonel Richard Henderson, was the best-organized and most ambitious of any of the competitors and had a large group of constituents lined up. The company grant—purchased from the Cherokee at Sycamore Shoals for ten thousand pounds—comprised nearly all of Kentucky. Colonel Henderson tried in the councils of Virginia and North Carolina, as well as in the Continental legislature, to make his huge tract a "colony" owned and run by his

company. The state governors objected, and John Adams's
diary notes:

"These proprietors have no grant from the Crown, nor from
any Colony; are within the limits of Virginia and North Carolina by their charters. . . . They are charged with republican
notions and Utopian schemes."

But even though they faced plenty of troubles in consolidat-
ing the company's enormous "grant," Colonel Henderson and
his partners pressed on with their plans, allotting various properties and homesites to the settling folk who had agreed to
become customers. There was momentarily some slight hope
for peace with the Indians, since the Battle of Point Pleasant in
October, 1774. Though Chief Cornstalk with his Mingo, Shawnee, and Wyandotte warriors had defeated the Virginians under
General Andrew Lewis in that engagement, the Indians seemed
to be discouraged and accepted one of the many peace treaties
hopefully arranged by the whites.

Throughout the years, Daniel Boone had made many a trip
into Kentucke, and though he fully expected Indian hostility
to boil up again and again, he was deeply interested in starting
pioneer settlements in the Great Valley, and felt sure they
would eventually be successful. Knowing the country so well, he
was the natural choice of Colonel Henderson as trail blazer for
the pack trains already assembling for the journey.

Boone with some thirty men cleared and marked a wagon-
track road from Cumberland Gap to a point on the Kentucky
River where Boonesborough was founded in the spring of 1775.
Incoming parties were made uneasy by groups who had given
up the struggle against Indians and were straggling back to
Virginia, and Boone, after leading in a large pack train from
the Transylvania Company, wrote Colonel Henderson on April
1, 1775, urging him to follow immediately as they had planned.

"My advice to you, sir, is to come or send as soon as possible.

Your company is desired greatly, for the people here are very uneasy, but are willing to stay and venture their lives with you, and now is the time to flusterate the intentions of the Indians and keep the country whilst we are in it."

Quotations from Boone's remarks and letters, set down by early scribes, nearly always needed and received brushing up as to spelling and grammar, but the gist of his meanings is usually quite as clear as his own well-known "D. Boone cilt a bar on this tree 1761." With very little "book-larnin'," he was a superior engineer as his maps, surveyed roads, and planned forts proved. His ideas on frontier law were farsighted and practical, his dealings and strategy with the Indians unique. So compelling were the legends of his courage and ability that even a rumor that he was on his way to help was enough, more than once, to put new spirit and hope into the harried defenders of some small beleaguered pioneer stockade. And certainly his April letter brought results.

Colonel Henderson's journal notes that in April he "arrived at Fort Boone at the mouth of Otter Creek, Cantucky River, where we were saluted by a running fire of about 25 guns, all that were then at the fort. The men appeared in high spirits." And later: "For want of obligatory law . . . our game soon . . . was driven off very much. As short a distance as good hunters thought of getting meat was 15 or 20 miles; nay sometimes . . . thirty miles, though by chance, once or twice a week, buffalo was killed within 5 or 6 miles of the camp. The wanton destruction of game gives great uneasiness."

A May entry reads: "Behind my camp about 50 yards from the river . . . stands one of the finest elm trees that perhaps nature has ever produced situated on a beautiful plain surrounded by a turf of fine white clover. The trunk is about 4 feet through to the first branches which are about 9 feet from the ground. . . . The diameter of the [spread] branches is 100 feet, and every fair day it describes a semicircle on the heavenly green around it, of upwards of 400 feet in circuit ... 100 persons may commodiously seat themselves under the branches. ... This divine tree ... is to be our church, and council chamber."

On May 23 delegates assembled there from Harrodsburg, Boiling Springs, St. Asaph, and Boonesborough settlements, "pleased with their Stations and in great good humor." After divine service by the Reverend John Lythe, Colonel Henderson opened the convention with a lengthy speech, flowery enough to found the school of silver-tongued orators long to flourish in Kentucky. A short excerpt:

"You are called and assembled at this time for a noble and an honorable purpose—a purpose, however ridiculous or idle it may appear at first view to superficial minds, yet is of the most solid consequence; and if prudence, firmness and wisdom are suffered to influence your councils and direct your conduct, the peace and harmony of thousands may be expected to result from your deliberations. ... You perhaps are fixing the palladium, or placing the first cornerstone of an edifice, the height and magnificence of whose superstructure is now in the womb of futurity, and can only become great and glorious in proportion to the excellence of its foundation."

In the years soon to follow, when claims and counterclaims of Kentucke land were thrashed out in court, a certain land agent spoke of a pioneer crowd—less high-spirited than this first council meeting, though many of the same men were present—as "a set of scoundrels who scarcely believe in God or fear a devil—if we are to judge from most of their looks, words, or actions."

After the colonel's speech had been answered with equal grandiloquence the convention got down to business, passing as its first law the establishment of courts of judicature. This was followed by a motion for regulating the militia and then Daniel Boone brought in a bill for the preservation of game and was appointed one of a committee of three to see that the law was carried out.

Other acts related to the punishment of criminals, the prevention of swearing and Sabbath-breaking (this one suggested by the preacher, naturally), writs of attachment, ascertaining clerks' and sheriffs' fees, and (again at Boone's suggestion) improving the breed of horses, this last of which was followed by the act of his brother, Squire Boone, for preserving the range.

All these bills were read three times and voted on by the assemblage and all were passed. Colonel Henderson then exhibited his title deed "from the Aborigines and first owners of the soil in Transylvania and attended by John Farrow, attorney for the head warriors or chiefs of the Cherokee Indians, who in presence of the Convention, made livery and seizin of all the lands in a deed of feoffment, then produced and bearing the date of March last, 1775." Following this, a contract of eighteen articles was entered into, including such matters as an annual election of delegates, the fact that the land office should always remain open and that there should be "perfect religious freedom and general toleration—provided, that the propagators of any doctrine or tenets, evidently tending to the subversion of our laws, shall for such conduct be amenable to, and punished by the civil courts."

It was then ordered that the delegates of Boonesborough be constituted a committee to see that the bills "be transcribed in a fair hand into a book," and the convention adjourned. Whatever dreams of empire the Transylvania Company may have had (and dreams of empire were very much the order of the day, the Transylvania Company simply being "personally conducted" and better organized than its competitors) came to nothing and the company failed within the following year. The temper of the settlers, whether they had come to the new country on their own or under the Transylvania aegis, was exceedingly independent, and there was much resentment over the company's proprietorship and the rising price of land.

Collins's definitive *History of Kentucky* makes it fully clear. "They who were already in the land, who had spied it out and were revelling in its luxuries, would be hail-fellows-well-met with the lordly Transylvanians, but acknowledge their superior rights and pay them tribute, NEVER! They would help them open the country, combine with them for defense, counsel with them for common safety and the common good, meet them for any purpose upon equal terms, but submit to them as lords of the soil, entitled to an annual quit-rent, NEVER!"

√ *George Rogers Clark and the Hair Buyer*

At this period, Kentucke Country had no recognized status as a part of Virginia. The mother state had her own hands full as the Revolutionary movement came to a crisis, but young George Rogers Clark, "genius of the frontier," was determined that Kentucky be accepted as a county of Virginia, entitled to some protection against the increasing Indian attacks, or established as an independent colony. He took the matter to Governor Patrick Henry and to the Virginia council of state. This body grudgingly offered young Clark a personal loan of five hundred pounds of gunpowder, which he curtly refused by letter. Unless Virginia assumed some responsibility toward her own western territory, and would therefore willingly *supply* (not give or loan) the powder for its protection, she could keep it!

Virginia finally met these terms and, in December, 1776, officially designated Kentucky a county. It was remarkable that Clark and his friend and fellow delegate, Gabriel Jones, ever got the gunpowder to Kentucky, for it was delivered at Pittsburgh, and the entire north Ohio Valley was alive with Indian agitation. The British Lieutenant Governor Hamilton (the Hair Buyer, so called because he was said to have offered a scalp bounty) was in charge of Detroit, and was driving a body blow against American insurrection by urging the Indians to wipe out the Kentucky forts and settlements.

This the Indians were delighted to try to do, and they burned, killed, and terrorized with enthusiasm. Jones and some others were killed getting the precious gunpowder to Harrodsburg, and the Indian attacks increased. On the old principle that offense is the best defense, Clark besought Governor Patrick Henry of Virginia to give him men, boats, and ammunition to overthrow the powerful British-held forts of Kaskaskia, Cahokia, and Vincennes, and thus discourage their Indian allies.

The Virginia assembly then gave the new Lieutenant Colonel Clark the money for his military needs, authorized a Kentucky land bonus as a reward for volunteers, and gave him secret instructions to take the British forts if he could, though his public orders mentioned only the raising of troops for the protection of Kentucky.

So it was that Louisville was born. Clark with volunteers from Pennsylvania way—some one hundred and fifty of them —as well as a number of "settling folk," left Redstone Old Fort in the spring of 1778 and floated down the Ohio to the Falls, making camp and starting the station on Corn Island.

The embattled Kentucky settlements couldn't spare many recruits for Clark's daring Northwest Expedition, but Simon Kenton, one of the great scouts of the day, with twenty men, did join up. A company of Virginians met Clark at the Falls, and on June 24 the trek began. With brilliant strategy, Clark used his small force to take Kaskaskia, sent a wing under

Joseph Bowman to take Cahokia, and then conquered the formidable Vincennes. Hamilton regained Vincennes temporarily, but Clark managed with inferior numbers to retake it in 1779, thus breaking the British hold on the west and greatly aiding the cause of the American Revolution.

Hamilton and his men were Clark's prisoners of war. Some of these were paroled but a group of twenty-seven, which included Hamilton, was given a holdfast guard of a couple of officers and twenty-one men. These set out on their trip for the Falls of the Ohio (Louisville), supplied with pork and flour and a good supply of whisky, and after three weeks reached their destination, where they were "welcomed" by the forty-eight inhabitants of the town—eleven families, four bachelors, and one Negro slave, according to accepted count. This welcome took the form of gunfire which, the Redcoats noted, continued most of the day. They were hustled into a windowless cabin, the furniture of which was strictly limited to a few three-legged stools and a puncheon table and bunks covered with straw ticks and buffalo skins. There was a fireplace where the cooking could be done but the Hair Buyer apparently had an appetite for egg-puddin' pone, for he gave one of Louisville's first hostesses a quilt in exchange for a portion.

A couple of days later, Louisville's first "distinguished visitor" and his companions were marched off to Harrodsburg where they stayed for ten days and were well treated and provided with horses. From here they went to Logan's Fort where Hamilton is quoted as saying that the people did not seem to be well disposed toward them and they were "accosted by the females especially in pretty coarse terms." From there they were taken on toward Virginia and, in Williamsburg, put in dungeons in the jail with common criminals, and denied even such privileges as writing materials, which, seemingly, would have been of little use to them anyway since they were handcuffed.

Perhaps, by contrast, Louisville's hospitality seemed warm and friendly and one wonders if, when the British lieutenant governor returned to his homeland some two years afterward, he ever gave a thought to that corn bread and the Kentucky housewife, who was at that moment and for many years afterward, likely enough, sleeping under his fine quilt, perhaps with a faint twinge of conscience and the hope that her neighbors would not think her a "fellow traveler"!

Daniel Boone's defense of Boonesborough in 1778 was also a major blow for American freedom, for had this fort, where so many settlers turned to safety, fallen, the remnant of Kentuckians would surely have been scattered and driven out. Boone was an Indian captive, having been taken with twenty-eight other men while making salt at the lower Blue Licks. As an adoptee and friend of Chief Blackfish, he was able to hear whispers of the plans to vanquish Boonesborough. He escaped, made his way to the fort, prepared it for siege, and eventually won the day.

In back-to-the-wall fighting on their own ground, Kentucky frontiersmen were unequaled. But in organized campaigns against the Indians, toward the end of the Revolution (and in the bloody years following it), they had their troubles. Lacking Clark's rare military gifts, and having no appetite at all for taking orders from their own chosen officers, they made almost unbelievable mistakes, everybody blaming everybody else for them. Well accustomed, each man of them, to meeting personal crises and acting on his own decisions, isolated-farmer style, he was more of a lone wolf than pack wolf.

Torch and Tomahawk

The Battle of the Blue Licks in August, 1782, is a sad illustration. A large Indian force, harrying the neighborhood under British command, was making a nonchalant retreat. The Kentucky forces, hoping to punish them before they could get back across the Ohio to Indian country, stampeded their own officers and each other into a trap, though they were in the main excellent woodsmen and experienced Indian fighters. The Indians hid in a ravine and routed their pursuers disastrously. Daniel Boone, leader of one frontal attack, lost a son there, and many a valuable pioneer leader died in that ill-advised foray.

A "true account" of the hazardous average life of those days was found in an 1837 *Family Magazine or Abstract of General Knowledge,* published in Cincinnati, and widely read in Kentucky. The piece, Eli Taylor's "Wonderful Escape from Indians," eclipses any fiction writer's wildest dream. Our hero, James Morgan of Bryan's Station, Kentucky, had "built a cabin, deadened timber, laid a worm fence, and planted corn. . . ."

"It was the fifteenth day of August, 1782;—the sun had descended; a pleasant breeze played through the surrounding wood; the cane bowed under its influence, and the green leaves of the corn waved in the air; Morgan had seated himself in the door of his cabin with his infant on his knee; his young and happy wife had laid aside her spinning wheel and was busily engaged in preparing the frugal meal. . . .

"That afternoon James Morgan had accidentally found a bundle of letters, which he had read to his wife before he had taken his seat in the door. It was a correspondence in which they had acknowledged an early and ardent attachment for each other, and the perusal left evident traces of joy on the countenance of both; the little infant, too, seemed to partake of its parents' feelings by its cherub smiles and infantile caresses.

"While thus agreeably employed, the report of a rifle was heard, another and another following in succession. Morgan sprang to his feet, his wife ran to the door, and they simultaneously exclaimed: 'Indians!' "

Barring the door, Morgan urged his wife to conceal herself in a small dugout under the floor while he escaped with the baby to summon help. But "maternal anguish overcame her timidity, and she seized her babe, gazing silently upon it and pressing it to her agitated bosom.

" 'In the name of Heaven, Eliza, release the child or we shall all be lost,' begged the distracted husband in a soft imploring voice."

Eliza, in several hundred words, was hustled into the cellar, and James, strapping the baby in a bag on his back, leaped to the garret and broke out through the roof to the ground where the savages set upon him with knives and tomahawks. But "the robust and athletic Morgan got the ascendency and hurried off. He was pursued and a dog set on his trail, but operated upon by all the feelings of a husband and father, he moved with the speed of a hunted stag, and soon outstripped the Indians and shot the dog."

He left the baby at his brother's house near Lexington and, with the brother, started back home, finding his house in flames, burned almost to the ground.

" 'My Wife!' he exclaimed, as he pressed one hand to his forehead and grasped the fence with the other to support his tottering frame. He gazed on the ruin and desolation and sank exhausted to the earth. . . . Morning came—the bright luminary of Heaven arose—and still found him seated near the expiring embers. In his right hand he held a stick with which he was tracing the name 'Eliza' on the ground, his left hand was thrown over his dog that lay at his side, looking first on the ruin and then on his master with evident signs of grief."

Finding bones burned to ashes in the ruined house, the brothers "silently consigned them to Mother Earth" and departed.

A few days later, James took part in the Battle of the Blue Licks, in which the Indians were victorious and chased the whites back across the Licking River "six and thirty miles." James was in the rear guard "reflecting on the lost lovely object of his affections when he received a rifle ball in his thigh. . . . An Indian sprang upon him, seized him by the hair and applied a scalping knife.

"At this moment Morgan cast his eyes upward and recognized the handkerchief that bound the head of the savage as his wife's! This increased activity to fury, and with deathlike grasp he hugged the brute to his bosom and plunged his knife through the back." After the Indian expired, Morgan crawled away undiscovered and unscalped, an anxious spectator of the ensuing battle.

"By midnight the Indians retired, leaving the ground covered with the slain, crimsoned with blood that had warmed the heart and animated the passions of many a patriot and soldier.

"The pale glimmering moon shone on the mangled bodies, then a cloud enveloped all in darkness, giving additional horror to the feeble cries of the dying, rendering doubly appalling the coarse growl of the bear, the loud howl of the wolf, the shrill notes of the wildcat and the panther feeding on the dead and dying. . . .

"Morgan looked forward to his end with the apathy of despair. . . .

"A ferocious-looking bear covered with blood approached him; he silently commended his soul to Heaven, but the satiated animal passed by. Morgan was offering thanks for his preservation when the cry of a pack of wolves opened upon him, again awakening him to a sense of danger.

"He placed his hands over his eyes, awaiting his fate in silent agony. He heard a rustling in the bushes—steps approached—a cold chill ran over him.

"Imagination, busy, creative imagination was actively employed; death, the most horrible death awaited him; he would be devoured alive.

"He felt a touch—the vital spark was almost extinguished—the cold sweat ran down in torrents—his hands were forced from his face—the moon passed from under a cloud—his eyes involuntarily opened and he beheld—*his wife,* who in a scarce audible voice exclaimed, 'My husband! My husband!' and fell upon his bosom. . . ."

Eliza explained that the Indians in looting the Morgan cabin had found and drunk some spirits, one of their band being stabbed to death in the ensuing quarrel. Blood dripped through the floor boards to Eliza's hiding place and, believing it to be her dear James's, she had shrieked aloud and had thus been discovered and taken prisoner. Escaping when the Indians were engaged in battle, she had seen James's horse pass her hiding place, and had felt sure he lay wounded on the field and that she would find him. . . .

Throughout the Revolution and for a good many years afterward, Kentucky suffered terribly from Indian raids. Pioneers were pouring in through the Wilderness Road and down the Ohio—there were 73,000 inhabitants when Kentucky became a state in 1792—yet travel to the new country and life in it were extremely hazardous. Indians attacked incoming boats anywhere and everywhere along the five-hundred-mile stretch of the Ohio River Kentucky border, and it was estimated that more than 1,500 people were killed or carried off, and 20,000 horses and thousands of dollars' worth of property stolen or destroyed during the years 1783-1790 alone.

When Kentucky asked the federal government for help, several abortive expeditions were made by volunteer militia companies commanded by some exceedingly inefficient and weak officers, with great loss of life and no success whatever in controlling the Indians. After several such defeats, the Kentuckians were embittered and their faith in the new Union was badly shaken. President Washington then asked General "Mad" Anthony Wayne to head the western army, and this experienced soldier made careful preparation for his campaign. In midsummer, 1794, General Charles Scott of Kentucky led sixteen hundred mounted volunteers to join General Wayne and his some three thousand regulars, and on August 30, on the Maumee River, the Battle of the Fallen Timbers took place. The Indians were so badly defeated and demoralized that the threat of raids of any real consequence ended there and then. Kentucky could begin to breathe easy.

CHAPTER 5

A Horse, a Gun, and a Violin

"A Round of Frolicks"

*F*ROM THE VERY beginning, Kentuckians have loved and
welcomed entertainment in any and every form. The tensions
of danger, land lawsuits, and the problems of establishing a new
government during one of the great population booms of
history put special premium on each lighter moment. From
cockfights, which are said to flourish still, to spelling bees,
which were reported to have been exciting events even without
the stimulus of $100,000 prizes, there was fun for all.

As Butler's early *History of Kentucky* sums it up: "Every
young man I know has a horse, a gun, and a violin.... These
were the great instruments of amusement—at races, shooting
matches, squirrel hunts . . . and dancing parties. Society seemed
to be viewed as if it were intended for amusement alone....
There was a round of frolicks whenever the exigencies of the
crops did not forbid them, and every farmer's house was a home
for all and a temple of jollity."

A gun and a horse were, of course, necessities. But aside from
their value as transportation and in farm work, horses bred
for spirit, speed, and stamina were the special love and pride of

57

red-blooded or blue-blooded (or mixture thereof) Kentucky people.

This was partially due to the English background and attitudes of a great many pioneers. Too, it was soon clear that horses thrived here. Long before our early Kentuckian realized that there was any connection between contaminated water and typhoid fever, he was quite aware that the limestone under the pastures and in the water was salubrious indeed to his beloved horses.

Without horses and corn, a crop that developed much more quickly than wheat and could be planted several times in a season, the country could never have been opened and held as soon as it was. So it was quite natural that the state's reputation for fast horses, and whisky, an early by-product of all that corn, should be established. As far as beautiful women are concerned, Kentucky has had her share. It is possible, however, that the premium set on any unattached lady in a man's frontier world might have something to do with the legend.

Horse racing was certainly one of the earliest recreations of Kentucky, and one of her original laws had to do with the improvement of the breed. Though the year 1789 marked the first actual laying out of a public racecourse in the state—in Lexington, naturally—racing had already been popular throughout the country for years at Humbles' Paths (Harrodsburg) and on the streets of Louisville, Georgetown, Frankfort, and other towns. Lexington's long Main Street was a fine place to race, and even as late as the last years of the nineteenth century exciting personal contests between riders or drivers took place there, in spite of a stern city ordinance forbidding such goings-on, "because of the attendant peril to limb and property, the congestion of crowds, and the possibilities of riot" in case feeling ran over-high.

The first private race track in Kentucky Country was prepared, owned, and used by the intrepid Indian fighter William Whitley to train his own thoroughbreds and for private racing events. The Whitley House—now a state park and a particularly attractive museum—was one of the earliest (1787-94) brick houses to be built in Kentucky. Off the old Wilderness Trail near Stanford and Crab Orchard, the house stands on a commanding knoll, almost as lonely as it was when it was built.

The initials W W are cunningly built into the front wall of the house by using the glazed "headers" of bricks. Its high narrow windows—to keep Indians from looking in or shooting in—its "bins" into which the children were put to hide during Indian scares, its secret passage and stairway, its tiny "musket windows" on the third floor for protection of the household, all lay hold on the imagination of any visitor today.

The deep, cool walls, the fine old brass knobs and locks, the simple, sturdy woodwork and fine lines of the house bring back the brave past with startling force. And there in the front hall is William Whitley's famous powder horn with its spirited inscription:

"William Whitley, I am your horn,
The truth I love, a lie I scorn.
Fill me with the best of powder,
I'll make your rifle crack the louder.
See how the dread terrific ball
Makes Indians bleed and Tories fall,
You with powder I'll supply
For to defend your Liberty."

All along the original Wilderness Road one finds pioneer landmarks, but few are preserved as is the Whitley House. One neglected and abandoned one is the famous old tavern, the Jackson "Stand," built in 1795, a decade only after the bloody Indian massacre of the McNitt Company at Defeated Camp, a mile or so away. The Levi Jackson Wilderness Road State Park marks the old site of Defeated, where some twenty-four pioneers, victims of the massacre, lie in a common grave. But the staunch old "Stand," finally giving up to decay and depredation, is unmarked except by the defeat of time. . . .

There was no question whatever about the importance of his gun and his horse to any young Kentuckian of early times, or of the quality of his marksmanship or "horse sense." As far as his violin is concerned, the standards were less exacting, his technique the least of his worries. The first fiddles, however, with "harps," lutes, and dulcimers were very much a part of the pioneer's lighter moments. Ballads of Scotland, Ireland, and England, and a few French and German folk tunes were listened to and passed on, and many a toe-tickling dance tune was made up on the spot, or partially remembered or picked up from some traveler or peddler.

Kentuckians always have delighted in entertaining, past and present, and because of the climate—a long, long spring and fall added to the June-August stretch—tended to favor the out-of-doors. Hayrides, possum hunts, picnics, barge dances on the rivers, garden parties, singing "by the glimmer of the moon" in deckchairs on the terrace (or puncheon log-seats down in the yard, or benches in the vine-covered gazebo of the Victorian period) elide smoothly, over the hurrying years, linking past and present. . . .

One can smell the honeysuckle, get a whiff of charcoal steak or barbecued chicken, hear the tinkle of ice, a strain of music, for it is summertime again, and a beautiful, beautiful balmy Kentucky night, and the livin' is more than easy. Everybody outside the cemetery is on the porch, or in the garden, or strolling or driving along the river or in the park, or dancing on the terrace, or sitting and visiting, or sitting and thinking, or maybe just sitting. . . .

Kentuckians, themselves no mean forks or trenchermen, have long been accused of "putting the hospital in hospitality," according to certain visitors. Admittedly, a round of ladies' luncheons in the Bluegrass state, replete with such famous dishes as cucumbers broiled in cream and butter, brandied sweet potatoes, huge fluffy chicken croquettes enriched with calves' brains and double cream (that float off the plate but leave a grease spot in the air), cobblers, hot biscuits, spoon bread, bourbon balls, *et al*, presents a challenge either in self-control or endurance.

Kissin' Kin

The "social climate" of Kentucky has been called warm and friendly, stand-offish and snobbish, indifferent, welcoming, cosmopolitan, and provincial, quite probably with justification, depending on the person, place, and viewpoint. Like any society developed on the American scene, Kentucky's grew from the simple to the complex, cherishing for generations the quaint idea that a newcomer is still a newcomer after twenty years' residence. But friends of friends and "kissin' kin" however distant belong right away, from whatever point of the compass they happen to hail.

Actually Kentucky Country, the first picket in the gateway west, is a gateway to all four directions. To the East she is to her annoyance still "West." To the true West she is practically "Down East." To the Deep South, also to her annoyance, she is North or Middle West. To the North she seems to be a melange of watermelons and magnolias, dueling pistols and juleps.

Being in the middle, and affected by the vastly different ways and attitudes surrounding her, but being also geographically separate, she has over the years developed her particular identity. Sentimentally but not professionally Southern, Kentucky is made of independent rather than defensive individuals, who squabble over everything in the category except their bred-in-the-bone pride in their lovely land.

As to the people who constituted her original warp and woof, there were wide social and educational differences. Some were the simplest of backwoodsmen, some were younger sons of established Colonial or European families, some had crossed the Ridge to escape the long arm of the law, some were men of property, some slaveholders, some had themselves been bondsmen. But except for the restless wanderers drawn always toward distant fields, the early Kentuckian, prince, peasant, or pauper, respected, loved, and longed to possess all the good land he could get his hands on and to enjoy it to the fullest.

Before the advent of more sophisticated pleasures, everybody in a neighborhood ordinarily turned out for almost any social event—a quilting bee or husking bee, perhaps, a candy pull, a squirrel hunt, a hoe-down, a "sing," or a wedding celebration and feast. Collins gives us a lively description of a big wedding, in the Bluegrass of stockade days.

Linsey-Woolsey Wedding

"On the morning of the wedding day, the groom and his attendants assembled at the house of his father, for the purpose of proceeding to the mansion of his bride, which it was desirable to reach before noon, the usual time of celebrating the nuptials. . . .

"Let the reader imagine an assemblage of people, without store, tailor, or mantua-maker within a hundred miles . . . the gentlemen dressed in shoe-packs, moccasins, leather breeches, leggins, and linsey hunting shirt, and all home-made—the ladies

in linsey petticoats or linen bed-gowns, coarse shoes, handkerchiefs, and buckskin gloves. If there were any buckles, rings,
buttons, or ruffles, they were relics of old times. The horses
were caparisoned with old halters, old bridles and saddles, a
rope or string as often constituting a girth as a piece of
leather. . . .

"The march [to the bride's mansion] was often interrupted
by obstructions . . . these difficulties often increased by the
jocularity and sometimes by the malice of the neighbors by
felling trees and tying grapevines across the way. Sometimes an
ambuscade was formed, and a discharge of several guns took
place so as to cover the wedding party with smoke, with a spring
of the horses, shrieks of the girls, and the chivalric spring of
their partners to save them from falling. . . .

"Another ceremony took place before the party reached the
house of the bride, after whisky was introduced, which was at
an early period. When the party had arrived within a mile of
the house, two young men would single out to run for the
bottle. The worse the path the better, as obstacles afforded an
opportunity for the greater display of intrepidity and horseman-
ship. The start was announced by an Indian yell; logs, brush,
muddy hollows, hills and glens were speedily passed by the
rival ponies. The bottle was always filled for the occasion, and
the first who reached the door was presented with the prize,
with which he returned in triumph to the company. The con-
tents of the bottle were distributed among the company.

"The ceremony of the marriage preceded the dinner, which
was a substantial backwoods feast of beef, pork, fowls and sometimes venison and bear meat, roasted and boiled with plenty of
potatoes, cabbage and other vegetables. After dinner the dancing commenced, and generally lasted till next morning. The
figures of the dances were three- and four-handed reels, or
square sets and jigs.

"About nine or ten o'clock a deputation of young ladies stole off the bride and put her to bed. This done a deputation of young men, in like manner, stole off the groom and placed him snugly by the side of his bride. The dance still continued and if seats happened to be scarce, every young man when not engaged in the dance was obliged to offer his lap as a seat for one of the girls, and the offer was sure to be accepted. In the midst of this hilarity the bride and groom were not forgotten. Pretty late in the night someone would remind the company that the new couple must stand in need of some refreshments: 'Black Betty,' which was the name of the bottle, did not go alone. Sometimes as much bread, beef, pork and cabbage was sent along with her as would afford a good meal for half a dozen hungry men. The young couple were compelled to eat and drink more or less of whatever was offered them. . . .

"With all their rudeness, these people were hospitable, and freely divided their rough fare with a neighbor or a stranger, and would have been offended at an offer to pay. In their settlements . . . they lived, they worked, they sought entertainment; they fought and feasted or suffered together in cordial harmony. They were warm and constant in their friendships; but bitter and revengeful in their resentments."

The manly art of self-defense, practiced oftener to settle an argument than to display skill, still amounted to entertainment and attracted crowds of onlookers. The rough and rowdy rivermen who manned keelboats or thrashed the sweeps of the clumsy flatboats as they floated down-river with the current (and even sometimes bushwhacked the barges upstream by looping a towrope around a stump ahead and p-u-l-l-ing) were famous fighters, gouging being a specialty.

Mike Fink, usually the accepted and best-known prototype of those half-horse-half-alligator bullies, boasted long and loud that he could "out-shoot, out-drink, out-gouge, out-run, out-fight, out-slash, and out-shout" all comers. "Get your smoked glass out, folks, here comes Mike to dazzle your eyeballs. Cockadoodledoooo!" Colorful, brutal, impudent, and independent, the river roustabouts and stevedores kept Kentucky's water commerce moving, in spite of inroads by river pirates, notably the "Outlaws of Cave-in-Rock" near Cairo. And certainly their shooting and wrestling matches, their lifting and "heaving" contests, were rugged but popular entertainment, so long as the onlooker could watch an ear or nose bitten off, or an eye gouged out, without turning fainthearted and running for the marshal.

On the more civilized side of the picture, the river towns enjoyed the delights of visits from theater flatboats with their "floating players," who performed, afternoons and evenings, many "enlightening and uplifting dramas." Louisville was so fond of the stage that after several temporary tents and sheds had proved inadequate, her citizens built a permanent playhouse in 1811. This was remodeled soon afterward by Samuel Drake, one of the first impressarios of the valley, into a fine three-story brick amphitheater with a pit, a tier of boxes, and a gallery.

Strolling players visited Lexington regularly, from 1797 on. Traveling wax galleries were also popular amusement attractions throughout the country. Lexington's specially built auditorium, completed before the turn of the eighteenth century, offered "regular dramatic performances and exhibitions of musical art," and circuses and carnival shows thrived in the New West, wherever they set up shop.

Audubon Goes to a Barbecue

But of all the forms of entertainment, public or private, and entered into by everybody, whatever his tastes or qualifications, the big elaborate (often political) barbecue with all its ramifications was by far the most exciting. When these affairs were private, so keen was the disappointment of the neglected that certain forms of revenge were indulged in. Refreshments would disappear, horses' tails and manes would be horridly trimmed while their owners were "partyfying," and now and again the unbidden would overlook the oversight and appear. A couplet of the day, source unknown, caused much amusement and speculation.

> *"There was a young man so benighted*
> *Who never knew when he was slighted.*
> *He'd go to a party and eat just as hearty*
> *As if he'd been really invited."*

Surely the most romantic and delightful picture of Kentucky hospitality ever presented was drawn by Audubon when he describes a Fourth of July barbecue which was held in the early 1800's on the shores of Beargrass Creek near Louisville.

It was hot as Kentucky midsummer days are almost sure to be but the company assembled under the welcome shade of the "majestick" beechwoods. Nearby a flock of sheep "ruminated on their grassy beds" and an air of repose hung over the scene.

"The free, single-hearted Kentuckian, bold, erect and proud of his Virginian descent, had, as usual, made arrangements for celebrating the day of his country's Independence. The whole neighborhood joined with one consent. No personal invitation was necessary where everyone was welcomed by his neighbor, and from the governor to the guider of the plow all met with light hearts and merry faces. Here the sun was bright in the clear blue sky. With flowers and birdsong and dancing butter-flies, the scene is idyllic and Columbia's sons and daughters seemed to have grown younger that morning.

"During the preceding week many servants and some masters had been busy clearing the area which was now a sylvan pavilion. Under the trees stood the wagons loaded with provisions. Each denizen had freely given his ox, his ham, his venison, his turkeys and other fowls. Here were to be seen flagons of every beverage used in the country. La Belle Riviere had opened her finny stores; the melons of all sorts, peaches plums and pears, would have sufficed to stock a market. In a word, Kentucky, the land of abundance, had supplied a feast for her children.

"A purling stream gave its waters freely while the gracious breezes cooled the air. Columns of smoke from the newly kindled fires rose above the trees; fifty cooks or more moved to and fro as they plied their trade; waiters of all qualities were disposing the dishes, the glasses and the punch bowls, amid vases filled with rich wines.

"Old Monongahela filled many a barrel for the crowd. And now the roasting viands perfume the air, and all appearances conspire to predict the speedy commencement of a banquet such as may suit the vigorous appetite of American woodsmen. Every steward is at his post, ready to receive the joyous groups that at this moment begin to emerge from the dark recesses of the woods.

"Each comely fair one, clad in pure white, is seen advancing under the protection of her sturdy lover, the neighing of their prancing steeds proclaiming how proud they are of their burden. The youthful riders leap from their seats, and the horses are speedily secured by twisting their bridles round a branch.

"As the youth of Kentucky lightly and gaily advanced towards the Barbecue they resembled a procession of nymphs and disguised divinities. Fathers and mothers smiled upon them, as they followed the brilliant cortege. In a short time the ground was alive with merriment. A great wooden cannon, bound with iron hoops, was now crammed with home-made powder; fire was conveyed to it by means of a train, and as the explosion burst forth, thousands of hearty huzzas mingled with its echoes. From the most learned a good oration fell in proud and gladdening words on every ear, and, although it probably did not equal the eloquence of a Clay, an Everett, a Webster or a Preston, it served to remind every Kentuckian present of the glorious name of Washington. Fifes and drums sounded the march which had ever led him to glory, and as they changed to our celebrated Yankee Doodle Dandy, the air rang with acclamations.

"Now the stewards invited the assembled throng to the feast. The fair led the van, and were first placed around the tables, which groaned under the profusion of the best productions of the country that had been heaped upon them. On each lovely nymph attended her gay beau, who, in her chance or sidelong glances ever watched an opportunity of reading his happiness. . . . Many a national toast was offered and accepted and many essayed an amicable reply. The ladies then retired to booths that had been erected at a little distance, to which they were conducted by their partners, who returned to the table, and having thus cleared for action, recommenced a series of hearty rounds. However, as Kentuckians are neither slow nor long at their meals, all were in a few minutes replenished, and after a few more draughts from the bowl, they rejoined the ladies, and prepared for the dance.

"Double lines of a hundred fair ones extended along the ground in the most shady part of the woods, while here and there smaller groups awaited the merry trills of reels and cotillions. A burst of music from violins, clarionets and bugles gave the welcome notice, and presently the whole assemblage seemed to be gracefully moving through the air. The 'hunting shirts' now joined the dance, their fringed skirts keeping time with the gowns of the ladies, and the married people of either sex stepped in and mixed with their children. Every countenance beamed with joy, every heart leaped with gladness, no pride, no pomp, no affectation were there; their spirits brightened as they continued their exhilarating exercise, and care and sorrow were flung to the winds. During each interval of rest refreshments of all sorts were handed round and, while the fair one cooled her lips with the grateful juice of the melon, the hunter of Kentucky quenched his thirst with ample draughts of well-tempered punch.

"I know, reader, that had you been with me on that day, you would have richly enjoyed the sight of this national fete champetre. You would have listened with pleasure to the ingenious tale of the lover, the wise talk of the elder on the affairs of state, the accounts of improvement in stock and utensils, and the hopes of continued prosperity to the country at large and to Kentucky in particular. You would have been pleased to see those who did not join the dance, shooting at distant marks with their heavy rifles, or watched how they showed off the superior speed of their high-bred spirited horses, while others recounted their hunting exploits, and at intervals made the woods ring with their bursts of laughter. . . .

"But now the sun has declined and the shades of evening creep over the scene. Large fires are lighted in the woods, casting the long shadows of the living columns far along the trodden ground, and flaring on the happy groups, loath to separate. In the still clear sky begin to sparkle the distant lamps of heaven. One might have thought that Nature, herself, smiled on the joy of her children. Supper now appeared on the tables and after all had again refreshed themselves, preparations were made for departure. The lover hurried for the steed of his fair one, the hunter seized the arm of his friend, families gathered into loving groups and all returned in peace to their happy homes. . . ." (*Family Magazine,* 1837)

CHAPTER 6

State of the Union

"Cinderella"

THE "HAPPY HOMES of the single-hearted, Virginia-proud Kentuckians" were often threatened by unclear titles, and the early law courts were hopelessly congested. Before Kentucky became a state, all cases of appeal had to be referred to Virginia, a thoroughly inconvenient and tedious proceeding, after endless bickering at home.

Original royal or colonial grants, Revolutionary bonuses, land-company sales, staked claims whether properly registered or not, infringed on each other in part or in whole in cat's-cradle confusion. On fine parchment deeds, boundary lines were often described as "½ mile from the oak split by lightning" or "following the bend of Petty's creek" or making use of some similar landmark that changed or disappeared entirely within a few years.

Surveyors were employed, but their surveys didn't always agree with earlier maps and plots. Newcomers were arriving every week to take possession of lands for which they had proof of ownership, only to find them already "proven" to belong to somebody else.

The matter of taking a case to Virginia for final settlement meant weeks of travel on rough and dangerous roads beset with trace bandits and harassed by Indians. It also meant costly delay, as the Virginia courts were too busy with their own full dockets to be in a hurry to take up the touchy problems of the distant "rampaging frontier."

Virginia, the dear mother state, professed much concern for Kentucky, but actually treated her like an unwelcome stepchild, keeping an iron maternal hand on her chiefly because the brat had been born with that silver spoon in its mouth. Among the rules she made for Kentucky to follow was one forbidding chasing maurauding Indians home to punish them, after they came up from the south or down from the north to kill, burn, and plunder. As in hopscotch or prisoners' base, it was fair to tag them on home ground, but when Colonel Benjamin Logan and General George Rogers Clark led retaliatory raids into Indian country, Virginia rebuked them.

Actually these punitive raids weren't at all successful, but it made Kentucky furious that these two heroes were called down for trying. And though Thomas Jefferson, too, was a great figure to Kentucky generally, the Old Dominion was becoming more and more unpopular as arbiter of the district's fate. She enjoyed the prestige of owning the great "western" tract, collected taxes from it, and gave out lands to her Revolutionary soldiers in lieu of back pay. But help Kentucky protect herself? Dear me, no!

The old saw—"a selfish mother makes a devoted child"— must have more than a grain of truth in it, because, though Kentucky grumbled and fretted, many of her people defended and clung to Virginia. Certainly they used kid gloves in dealing with her, sending one polite petition after another, which she laid aside after patting a light yawn. Yet in spite of her indifference, and a sizable number of Kentuckians hailing from other seaboard states, it would be hard today to find anybody who has lived here long enough to get his television set adjusted whose family tree doesn't boast a root or so in the Old Dominion.

The only bitter argument of recent times, so far as we know, was one that raged a few years back on the controversial subject of juleps. Naturally both states claimed the invention of the drink, and the *Louisville Courier-Journal* and the *Richmond Post Dispatch* did the jousting, never settling the question of crushing mint. In Richmond, it seems, they mash the mint and sip their fragrant juleps in book-lined libraries beside the "glowing embers of a beechwood fire." Since Kentucky greenery —whether or not it gets mashed—usually grows in the summertime, the *Courier* asked trenchantly: "What do you use for mint?" And Mother V., nodding by those glowing embers, didn't bother to say. It could be that she inclined toward the *Courier's* famous Marse Henry Watterson recipe. "Select tender mint, make a simple syrup, crush some ice, throw all of this away and take your bourbon straight."

Cutting Virginia's Apron Strings

Back in the 1780's *The Kentucky Gazette* of Lexington carried the first arguments on the question of cutting Mom's apron strings. Opinion was naturally divided. Many called the move premature and dangerous. But Kentuckians were well accustomed to dangers of all kinds. And who knew what was best for Kentucky's future?

Hating the British heartily, delighted that the winter of 1783 saw the Revolution won and the troops of the Crown sailing drearily homeward from New York Harbor, Kentucky was still skeptical about the new Confederation of States being formed. During the next several years the original thirteen colonies had so much trouble getting together on a national government, that any hope for help to solve Kentucky's problems seemed silly.

With her rich resources and fertile lands she was soon producing salable export goods by the barrel, bale, and bargeload. The Spanish port of New Orleans was the perfect market. The awkward broadhorns and keelboats of the time could, with backbreaking labor, be thrashed upstream with trade cargo, but it was as simple as one-two-three to float ten times as many of the big flats and barges down to New Orleans, sell the cargo for local, seaboard, or European trade, and auction the barges off for their construction timbers or firewood value.

When Spain closed the big gulf port, as she did from time to time, Kentucky was desperate. Wily and ambitious General James Wilkinson, friend of the Spanish Colonial Governor Miro, urged a Kentucky alliance with Spain. Whether he wanted to see his homeland annexed or preferred setting up a personal empire in the New West was never made fully clear. But the deal he tried to make smelled decidedly fishy, and the Kentuckians balked.

It was John Jay, Secretary of Foreign Affairs in 1785, who raised frontier blood to the boiling point. In dickering with the minister from Spain for a favorable trade treaty for the nation, he suggested rewarding Spain with a thirty-year right to control the vital Mississippi River! Congress didn't agree to this, but the sting of the thing festered for years in the river valleys.

Kentucky was shocked by her own helplessness. Clearly, she was a pawn for the notionate infant government to play with. Infuriated by new taxes—especially the one on bourbon whisky —and dependent on the Mississippi trade, many a leader far more conscientious than Wilkinson urged a separate alliance with Spain.

As the 1780's neared an end, other leaders pressed the idea

of full independence for Kentucky. By and large, Kentucky people were young people, no native-born person being beyond teen age. Everybody, original and newcomer alike, was ready for a change. But since there was nothing in bloodstreams or customs compatible with Spain, and because level heads managed to prevail, Kentucky decided at a series of conventions at Danville to ask to join the Union and have a voice in affairs.

Virginia finally gave her blessing, in the form of several Enabling Acts, on Kentucky's separation, and Congress after much indifference and delay voted in 1791 to admit Kentucky, whenever she could present an acceptable constitution.

Actually this was only two years after the first presidential election in the United States, Washington having been chosen for the office in February, 1789, five years and two months after he resigned his commission as commander in chief of the Continental Army.

The Fifteenth Stripe

Though Kentucky made petition to become a state before Vermont did, she was slow to draft her constitution, and Vermont was made the fourteenth state in 1791. Kentucky won the fifteenth stripe on the flag in June, 1792. (Later, additional stars superseded stripes, which were reduced to the original thirteen.) She had the satisfaction of being told by President Washington and the Congress that her constitution and bill of rights were brilliant and thoughtful. Certainly these documents were as democratic as the men who wrote them could make them, guaranteeing political equality, freedom of religion, press, election, person, house, and papers, the right to bear arms in self-defense and in defense of the state, neither church membership nor property ownership to affect voting privilege, no confiscation of suicides' estates, fair jury trial for anyone accused of crime, and no man except government employees and militia members to be subject to military trial, and many other protections of personal liberties.

Strangely enough, and in spite of opposition from ministers of several churches, point nine of the constitution assured the practice of slavery. Not only that, but the law stipulated that the legislature pass no future laws to interfere with it.

The year 1792 brought news of the French Revolution and the guillotining of hundreds of royalists. Tom Paine was writing his *Age of Reason*. Napoleon was a young officer in Paris. America was three hundred years old. (In 1492 you know who sailed the ocean blue.)

In Massachusetts that year (*1792*—not 14) , the first cracker bakery was put in operation. Rickett's Circus, first big top in the Western hemisphere, opened in Philadelphia, with George Washington on hand to enjoy it.

A factory in Massachusetts was making the first window glass in quantity in the country. The life expectancy (at birth) of a young American man was thirty-five years, of a young woman, thirty-seven. There were about 35,000 inhabitants of New York City, some 45,000 of Philadelphia. Chicago wouldn't be born for another forty-five years.

There were more than 750,000 people in Virginia, and fewer than 75,000 in Kentucky. Maysville (old Limestone) near Cincinnati, on the Ohio, was Kentucky's biggest entry port. There were about four hundred people in Louisville. Frankfort, a tiny little town on the Kentucky, tucked into a valley between surrounding hills, had won her fight to be the new capital. In this very year of 1792, the town and Franklin County around it suffered a particularly bloody hit-and-run attack from a band of Indian warriors over a hundred strong.

Nine-tenths of Kentucky Country was still wild, in spite of the growing settlements and the constant arrival of adventurous young immigrants. With Indians on the loose, and outlaws on river and trace, the established towns had schools—even dancing schools. Theaters, a budding university, boot makers, tailors, an "institute of Singing and Psalmody," a great many churches, and other accoutrements of civilization were flourishing.

Isaac Shelby, First Governor of Kentucky

To head this new state, with all its inner contrasts and violent differences, a very great man was chosen, Isaac Shelby. Certainly he had every qualification. He had fought the Indians and staked his own land claim near Danville in 1775, and had gone back over the mountains to serve in the Revolution, becoming the hero of King's Mountain, leading his men there in a decisive victory over the British. In 1783 he had married Susannah Hart, daughter of Nathaniel Hart of the Transylvania Company, a brave and respected gentleman who, like many another, met his death by tomahawk near Boonesborough.

Isaac Shelby had served with distinction at the Danville Constitutional Conventions, and was a man everyone liked personally—quite an achievement in those parlous times. His first concern as governor was to free Kentucky from the continuing Indian menace, but before this could be fully accomplished another crisis boiled up.

In the first year of Shelby's term, Edmond Genêt came to Kentucky, sent to America by the French republic to stir up the country against Spain, a major enemy of France. One would have thought, glancing back over the unremitting bloodshed Kentucky Country had experienced from its inception, that this might have been an impossible assignment. But not at all. The Kentuckians resented the way the Spanish dominated the Mississippi, naturally. Too, Spain was a monarchy like England, and France was a republic.

It seems to have been no trouble at all for Genêt and his helpers to work up a strong interest in a Kentucky expedition to fight Spain at New Orleans. Of course only a few years ago many Kentuckians had been ready for a Spanish alliance, but memories and tempers were short—and perhaps those who now wanted to fight Spain never had liked her anyway.

Advised strongly by President Washington not to allow this war on Spain to start, Governor Shelby steered a careful course. He could, he said, stop a mass invasion, but not the going down of small groups, for that would infringe on private liberties. Meantime he urged the Louisiana governor to open New Orleans.

This was done, Genêt was recalled to Paris, and all was momentarily well, as Kentucky once more put down her guns and polished up her plowshares.

CHAPTER 7

Reckon with the Rivers

Old Guns for New

*W*HEN KENTUCKY laid aside her guns she didn't lay them far from easy access. Even after General "Mad" Anthony Wayne just about finished the threat of big Indian raids in 1794, the Kentuckians who had gone north to help him came home with the uneasy knowledge that there were plenty of savages up there quite capable of rising again.

The Union, even after Kentucky had joined it, was far from being any Rock of Gibraltar of strength and authority, and still showed open partiality to the seaboard states. Like Topsy, Kentucky "just growed, and growed tremendous fast," pretty much as she pleased.

One of the personal liberties that Kentuckians exercised most assiduously seems to have been the "right to bear arms in self-defense." From duels on or off the field of honor, to "election shootin's," to bloody mountain feuds, that clause stretched conveniently. Kentucky Country's reputation for violence was justified for too many years, but its persistence sometimes annoys and often amuses present-day citizens, many of whom wouldn't know a muzzle-loader from an automatic pistol.

At Derby time a year or so ago, a Louisville hostess happened to be giving a small dinner party. It developed, when she was inviting her guests, that the guest of honor mentioned his collection of rare old guns. To compliment him and provide a conversation piece, the hostess asked a friend in town to bring a fine squirrel rifle from his own modest collection for the visiting fireman to see.

Obligingly the friend brought his whole collection, some six pieces. They were heavy, and when other guests arriving at the party saw him struggling with them, they offered to help him carry them in. He was parceling out rifles when an out-of-state car pulled up, nearby, comments therefrom ringing out delightedly.

"Look at that! Are those things *guns?"*

"Sure they're guns. You forget we're in Kentucky."

"You mean they go around with *guns* on their shoulders?"

"You see 'em, don't you?"

"But those women have on *evening* dresses. The men look perfectly all right—I mean, they're like anybody else—except—"

Fervently wishing for a coonskin cap or two, the gun-toters, keeping their faces as straight as possible, stalked solemnly in single file to the house. . . .

Long after Kentucky society had developed to the point where everybody looked like everybody else, and was enjoying all the niceties of thoroughgoing, well-polished civilization, there were plenty of backwoods localities where guns stacked at the door of meeting house or tavern caused no comment from anybody. These isolated spots in foothills or mountains existed where early settlers had left the buffalo-trail roads. Land transportation was miserably hard and slow in the early years. Even so, at the eighteenth century's turn, there were more than 200,000 people in the state by count, with some several too hard to find to be included.

Flatboats, Broadhorns, and Arks

This enormous expansion was made possible by the rivers that slice through Kentucky from the Big Sandy to the Mississippi. The Ohio, great natural waterway that it is, swept the boatloads of people along, peppering the shores with settlements. The tributaries—the Licking, the arterial Kentucky, the Salt, the Green and the Barren, the mighty Cumberland, and the final stretch of the Tennessee—all flowing north into the Ohio, laid open the heart of the wilderness to anybody with a flatboat, a strong back, and a spirit of adventure.

Long before the idea of steam was more than a simmer in the minds of its experimenters, the arks and broadhorns were bringing people in, floating Northern wares to them, and marketing Kentucky produce in quantity down-river.

Life was full of hazard, as in any great frontier move. Among the great numbers of immigrants descending on Kentucky were adventurers, the lawless, the vultures, the aimless wanderers. But at the same time came the home-loving, the law-abiding. Every kind and condition was represented—the ignorant backwoodsman, the scholar, the aristocrat, the trader, the professional man, and the artisan. This was unlike a gold rush or oil rush. Mushroom towns didn't spring up and die down to sprout again farther on. Once a root went down, a town usually grew, the center of the farming community around it, for farming was the real and true concern here, and the towns and cities were dependent on the land.

There was a permanent quality about the very materials available for building—staunch logs, clay suitable for brick making, abundant rock to be quarried, fieldstone in quantity. In contrast to this solidity, the flowing rivers promised an ever-changing scene and a future of development and surprise.

A number of people who floated downstream from the boat-yards of Redstone Old Fort, Pennsylvania, made use of the timbers of their flatboats in the building of their houses. The wise ones chose high ground, the river floods and shifts of channel being an ever-present threat. In some of the lovely old river houses today, enlarged and improved over the years, can be found the beautiful hand-hewn rafters and joists, puncheon floors, mantelpieces, and other examples of sturdy, mellowed woodwork, patiently fashioned during long-long-ago Redstone winters, while their makers waited for the spring floods to float the big arks down to the promised lands.

Sometimes in these serene old houses a few window panes, or perhaps a fan-light, of the original famous Pittsburgh glass have survived. A few old houses set too close to the water, flooded again and again, still haunt the river banks. But more familiar to today's waterline scene are the shacks, shantyboats, and ancient houseboats (floating or beached) where the true folk-of-the-river (many of them descended from the roustabouts and bullies of the old "glory days" of the flatboats and barges) live out their years. River rats, they are called, for they are shy and suspicious, existing in contented squalor, setting trotlines or putting out a few cane poles with a mat of hooks on a hemp string to snag a buffalo or catfish when they "take a notion." The despair of social agencies, most of them resent do-gooder interference, keeping as independent of the world around them as did their doughty forebears.

Half-Horse, Half-Alligator

In the first half century of Kentucky's history, the brawling, hard-drinking, violent half-horse-half-alligator boatmen did more than their part in giving the country her blood-and-

thunder reputation. Her gentler people were continually embarrassed by complaints and comments about these bullies, who
were often accepted by outsiders as typical. They were necessary to the handling of cargoes and the traffic of the river, however, though they demanded barrels of free whisky, a big share
of profits, and no questions asked. Brawny men, they could also
be shrewd in a bargain and tricky in a practical way.

One story about the redoubtable Mike Fink is concerned
with a flock of sheep belonging to a Louisville city father, too
well protected by local law to be openly fleeced. Mike sprinkled
a few fat woolies with sneezing snuff, convinced the owner that
they had anthrax, obligingly butchered them and hauled them
away, and gave one of the Gateway City's first big barbecues.

In the teeming flatboat era, as many as one hundred and fifty
down-drifting craft loaded with families, furniture, and farm
animals were known to have passed a given point in one day.
The keelboats, made for swifter travel, had partial sails and
trim sweeps to propel them. Some boats were galley-style, with
half a dozen sets of long oars. But the big arks and broadhorns
(often as a figurehead these boats were decorated with a wide
pair of horns or antlers) as well as flatboats and barges had only
the current to carry them along, though they were equipped
with poles, booms, fins, or a big sweep-thrash to keep them
headed in the right direction and to help them over shallow
spots.

The snags and sawyers (tree limbs caught in the bottom,
sawing the water), the deadheads (water-soaked logs hard to
see because they floated just under the surface) and rocky
shallows, sand bars and eddies were the natural river hazards.
The falls below Louisville—actually a series of rockshelves and
turbulent riffles—were quite difficult to navigate, and here the
rivermen were invaluable. They knew every rock in the channel

and could ease the floundering monster boats across with consummate strength and skill.

How to Scuttle a Boat

Though organized Indian raids were over during the biggest boom of the flatboat, there were still isolated cases of savage attack, and plenty of uneasiness about it in travelers' minds. More to be dreaded were the white fiends who operated the robbers' caves and hideouts along the lonely stretches of the river. The biggest concentrations of these outlaws were at Cave-in-Rock near Cairo, Illinois, and old Fort Massiac on the Ohio near the mouth of the Tennessee River. Using these two convenient locations as headquarters, gangs of thieves and murderers preyed up- and downstream on the boatloads of settlers. They did hijack freight cargoes from time to time, but freight being awkward to dispose of, they usually preferred the savings of a settler, and his wife's jewelry and finery as prizes.

A favorite way to make the work easy was to use a decoy, perhaps a wailing child begging for help, crying he was hurt or had escaped from Indians. The harder but surer way was to swim or row out to a passing flatboat at night, dive under the shallow-draft bottom, and pull the oakum out of the seams. The sleeping family would awake to the horror of a foundering boat and the knives of the bandits. The boat could be plundered, the owners and their families murdered, disemboweled, filled with rocks and gravel, and the whole enterprise sunk without a trace in an hour or so.

One satisfying story is the saga of a group of settlers who had been successful flatboaters themselves and were determined to revenge some of their friends who had been less lucky. Using an old ark as counter decoy, they floated past Fort Massiac, haunt of the vicious Colonel Plug (M. Fleuger from New Hampshire). Obligingly he tried to lure the ark to shore, and obligingly the ark responded, presenting the bandits with a taste of variety, for the boatmen were well armed and, in the fight that took place at once, a number of the gang were killed or taken prisoner. Plug himself, an expert torturer, was beaten up, tied to a tree in a swamp, and left for the mosquitoes to finish. Unhappily he was too tough for them and was rescued alive by his benighted wife. Later, however, he drowned while doing a regular night's work. The boat he was busy scuttling was caught in a sudden river storm, blowing too far out for the old wretch to be able to swim back to shore, his own men having rowed on to safety without him.

Mr. Burr Comes to Kentucky

Regardless of outlaws, Indians, and shoals, Kentucky was doing an enormous export business in between Mississippi blockades by the Spanish in New Orleans. Huge amounts of corn, cornmeal, flour, bourbon whisky, cider, apples, beef, pork, hides, pelts, ginseng, hemp, rope, gunpowder, salt, maple sugar, soap, and of course, tobacco, went down to the south, successfully and very profitably.

Then Spain suddenly ceded Louisiana to France, who sold it off in 1803 to the United States. New Orleans was included in this fabulous Louisiana Purchase. Nobody knew exactly the extent of the giant tract of land. It lay west of the Mississippi and stretched from the Gulf of Mexico to Canada and was bordered roughly by the Rocky Mountains, a bargain for $15,000,000, some said.

Kentucky was pleased, chiefly because New Orleans was American. The Eastern states were horrified. The great Ohio

Valley was enough of an indigestible lump for an infant nation to try to swallow, in their opinion, without adding enough to choke it. The seaboard press described the Purchase as "an impossible wilderness, one that can never be settled by Americans" (a viewpoint still current in certain sheltered circles, we find).

When word got around that Spain was questioning France's right to sell Louisiana, and that New Orleans might again "go Spanish," Kentucky was ready to call out the militia and march on Florida. The government discouraged this, but Aaron Burr, visiting in the Bluegrass, came very near bringing off such a move. He and his partner, the unscrupulous James Wilkinson, made plans to equip and man a river flotilla to go down and go after the Spanish holdings.

A number of prominent Kentucky leaders were drawn into the scheme in 1805, but a year or so later, when Burr on a subsequent Kentucky visit was accused of conspiracy and the intent to set up for himself a southwest republic, they prudently backed out. When Burr stood before the bar of justice in Frankfort, it was whispered that there was much uneasiness in high places lest the horrid word traitor, now attached in many minds to Burr, spread to others whose early enthusiasm for his ideas was now stone-cold.

Opinion was then and has always been divided over Burr's loyalty. Henry Clay, after looking pretty carefully into the fiasco—Burr had sailed with the flotilla and had been "turned in" to President Thomas Jefferson and to the Kentucky authorities by his untrustworthy partner, Wilkinson—agreed to be one of his lawyers. And certainly the Frankfort trials couldn't produce a conviction. Nor could those in Richmond, Virginia, later.

Meantime the little capital city of Frankfort on the Kentucky was socially torn asunder over the question of just how

Mr. Burr was to be treated in the free intervals between strung-out court sessions. It was well known that he was wanted in the East for the killing of Alexander Hamilton in that trumped-up duel. But dueling was commonplace in Kentucky. He was under the cloud of suspicion of treason, but he had not been proved guilty and probably wouldn't be.

Public opinion at this time was far from a united force in favor of the federal government, which was still looked on by many as a body determined to exploit the West and discriminate against it. Kentucky generally had been in sympathy with the Whisky Rebellion up Pennsylvania way and resented keenly the heavy tax on distilled spirits voted by Congress.

Kentucky people had no reason to think Mr. Burr was plotting against *Kentucky,* had they? After all he had visited Frankfort and Lexington and the surrounding Bluegrass before, and had been very well received. An ex-vice president, he was certainly a distinguished visitor and so deserved attention. Too, he was a man of high fashion and personal elegance, of great erudition and charm. . . .

Already enjoying both the practice and the reputation of hospitality, society felt it had to do *something.* And as Kentuckians naturally would do, they took sides. One daring young host and hostess gave a party in honor of Mr. Burr. Another party followed at once, this one ignoring the gentleman's existence and that of his known champions. After several of these pro-Burr and anti-Burr affairs, the story goes that an elaborate ball was planned (by which faction we are not at all sure) which sounded so beguiling that differences were forgotten. Mr. Burr, his investigators and defenders, and a comprehensive array of guests turned out from miles around, everybody in best bib and tucker, with dancing till midnight at a most successful affair.

The many frivolous quirks, such as this one, in Kentucky's

story can be viewed with sympathy when we consider the youthfulness of so much of her population at the time. This was not the age of the Victorian dowager, firmly esconced on a stout branch of a flourishing native family tree. Many a hardy young family came highly pedigreed, but many others didn't. They all swarmed in to the new world to make it theirs, establish themselves as advantageously as they could in every way, and have as much fun as could possibly be managed, and they met each new situation with great exuberance.

Elegant Wilderness

Though nobody realized it then, the era of steam was about to begin. In a little while paddle wheelers from New Orleans would be bringing in buttons and needles and silks and satins, toys and tools and silverware, ironwork, marble mantels, and gilded mirrors, books, objects of art, lace shawls, French dolls, spinets, carpets and furniture, rice, coffee, tea, molasses and *fine white sugar.* Sharp-eyed commission men and chin-whiskered, resplendent captains, as well as stevedores loading and unloading cargoes, would soon take the place of the strutting, "ondacious" river bullies whose kingship over the wharfs and banks of the big streams was toppling.

The growth of the river towns was notionate, and their treatment of the water highway that made them was shameful. Even now, though improvements have been demanded and enforced, sewage and factory waste still pollute the streams in many places, and once lovely stretches of waterfront are now unnecessarily ugly.

Still, as seen from the river, there is a certain stage quality of shore and skyline, from the backdrop of factory and railroad yard to well-groomed park. And the houses strung out along the high banks of the charming old towns from Catlettsburg to Hickman become enchanting. Maysville, rich old tobacco center, has a particularly beautiful façade, protected at last after many inundations by a $7,000,000 flood wall.

Louisville, the one and only metropolis of Kentucky, owes her early importance to her first big problem, the Falls of the Ohio, for it was the Portland Canal that drew the major traffic to the Kentucky side rather than the Indiana one. A fast-growing, highly industrial and cosmopolitan place, Louisville has been called a variety of names.

"The Gateway," "City of Homes and Churches," "An Old Museum Piece," "Casher-in on Culture," "City of Trees and Parks," "Derby Town," and so on. She is the center of Kentucky's big business, and is known too for her philharmonic orchestra and the new works commissioned by it and first performed here; for her high-powered public library, her important university, for her peaceful integration of schools, her Art Center, her Louisville Fund, her Speed Museum, and her giant new State Fair Grounds—and so on and on.

Here in Louisville Marse Henry Watterson wrote his famous editorials, Annie Fellows Johnston her beloved "Little Colonel" books, Alice Hegan Rice the universally enjoyed *Mrs. Wiggs of the Cabbage Patch,* Cleves Kinkead his long-time success *Common Clay,* George Madden Martin her humorous *Emmy Lou,* Eleanor Mercein Kelly her charming *Basquerie.* These are only a few examples of past achievements to which Louisville has long pointed with pride and affection. Currently Louisville also has a higher-than-average percentage of recognized authors, and her literary stream still flows on.

Follow the Ohio's stream on southwest to Henderson, and one finds a town languorous and pleasant of atmosphere, rich with history. It was founded in 1797 by Colonel Richard Henderson and his Transylvania Company after they compromised their earlier huge claim. Here Audubon lived for a number of years, sketching his famous birds and carrying on a small business.

Paducah, well down toward the Ohio-Mississippi confluence, has been called the "Capital of Western Kentucky." Established in 1827 by William Clark, brother of George Rogers and partner in the famed Lewis and Clark Expedition, it was named Paduke, for a chief of the Chickasaw. A typical big-little Kentucky town, it has attracted much outside notice because of its two sons, the late Senator Alben Barkley, familiarly known as the Veep, and Irvin S. Cobb, whose tales of Judge Priest with all his kin and friends made and still make fine hilarious reading.

A cousin of Cobb's is said to have remarked, "Of course *we* like Irvin's stories. But it seems mighty funny that anybody else would, because after all they don't even know the folks in them."

The very rivers that developed and enriched the land are often also her inimical foes. From the mountains to the valleys, many a town near a river has been devastated by flood again and again, although flood walls and a system of reservoirs hold out much hope that it can't happen here again. An old-timer, Cap Fuller, who sells minnows and rents john-boats near the Louisville waterfront, expressed the feelings of the real riverman:

"Oh sure, we seen a lot of high water around here, but there was just the one flood. When? Why, 1937, a course. My ole rockin' chair was left on top of a telegraph pole. An' you must a seen that fish they ketched in the Brown Hotel lobby—right smart perch. Broadway was a roarin' torrent and the river was ten mile wide of trash an' floatin' outbuildin's, busted houses and dead livestock. Water was threatenin' the bridges, an' eatin' out the banks, an' takin' over every town in its path. Them Gloucester fishermen come down, set their boats on that wild current on the Indiany side, and rowed across to help us. They was men, fer you! Everybody pitched in, an' somehow we come out of it. But if I git to Heaven, I'm goin' to have a yarn-spinnin' bout with ole man Noah, cause here in Kentucky our rivers don't do things by halves."

Indeed they don't, as the 1957 floods that devastated eastern Kentucky sadly proved!

CHAPTER 8

True Tales Are Tallest

KENTUCKIANS," a notable wit once quipped, "are just like other folks, only more so." And certainly a glance back over the politicking, orating, "lawing," dueling, adventuring yesterday of Kentucky men and women would seem to bear this out.

Take the mere matter of piling up the years. It's fairly evident that "Kentuckians never do things by halves" for a survey of the oldest burying grounds brings a twinge of sympathetic heartache at the number of babies and young people sleeping there, followed by startled amazement at the tenacious apples who clung to their family trees for very nearly a good round century.

Statistically Kentucky seems to have harbored more than her share of centenarians. In 1840, almost sixty years after the close of soldiering, more than eight hundred citizens who had fought in the Revolutionary War were still alive, over two-thirds of them active farmers, horse breeders (an old gentleman in Lexington is known to have died at the age of one hundred and four from the "results of a fall sustained while breaking a colt"), and heads of families. A Mr. Stufflebean and thirteen other veterans were well past the century mark.

In the early twentieth century, few state or county fairs were

TRUE TALES ARE TALLEST 93

complete without Uncle Johnny Shell, a true philanthropist in his home county, and very widely known. Uncle Johnny would set up a tent at the various fairs, and for a nominal (and sometimes free) admission allow the customers to gaze upon him, his ninety-year-old daughter, and five-year-old son (ages varying according to the date, naturally). It was fairly well established that Uncle Johnny was one hundred and twenty-one when that youngest son turned five.

About the same time Uncle Johnny became a real paying curiosity, Tiny Mite, too, was a popular Kentucky wonder—"The world's smallest horse, weighing even with a fox-terrier dog, and shod with genuine silver quarters."

The Wild Man from Borneo was always a Midway favorite, and caused a furore one year at the State Fair, when he was called to the telephone. He was in a hurry to get his message—telephone service from the fair office being a little unreliable at the time—and ran through the crowd in his scant costume, earrings, and a wild wig, with long sharp teeth fitted firmly over his own. Since people *wanted* to believe in the Wild Man, the contretemps was a serious one, and a new Wild Man had to be "Captured and Transported at Great Danger and Expense" to replace the tame one, the following year.

Considerably earlier, in 1841, little Miss Penelope Scott, age thirteen, of Leesburg, was a natural wonder with no fake about it. She was taken by her parents to Lexington for scientific examination, and "hundreds of citizens visited the wonderful little stranger, though no charge was made for admission." It seems that Miss Penelope's right thumb grew quantities of hair, four or five hairs from three to twenty-six inches long being shed in a day. Her physician, Dr. Carson Gibney, a graduate of Transylvania Medical School, was unable to explain the phenomenon or diagnose any disease, but there was no question as to the accuracy of the observations made.

Local Color

In 1833, one of the most disastrous plague years ever to be visited on Kentucky Country, the doctors resorted to every imaginable remedy and preventive, usually in vain. In Lexington over five hundred people died within three weeks. Barrels of pitch were burned on street corners to purify the air. A cannon was fired again and again to "break up plague-ridden clouds."

Nurses and visitors of mercy wore thin black masks as protection to themselves and others, and everyone who had been in an infected district was asked to blow a horn to warn others away. Garlic worn in the shoes was said to be a preventive. Calomel and sovereign waters, Royal Antidote and opium pills, bismuth and catechu were the chief remedies.

Food was scarce and people going to buy it dropped their silver money in a bucket of vinegar to protect the storekeeper from infection it might carry. The matter of grave-digging became an acute problem, and here one of Kentucky's strangest heroes distinguished himself. "King Solomon" (immortalized by James Lane Allen) was a town derelict, a white man, who had been sold as a debtor's chattel to a free woman of color. Of no account to anybody before this dreadful crisis, he dug graves day and night, when "better" men were leaving the cholera-ridden community as fast as they could. . . .

There are many local stories widely known and believed, substantiating details having been added where needed, one feels, when the various versions are heard. There is the story of the beautiful lady who died on the ballroom floor of long-ago popular Graham Springs Resort or Sanatorium in Harrodsburg, after dancing set after set in wild and graceful abandon. She was buried at once on the hotel grounds, and only the word

"Unknown" marks the gravestone, but many a romantic tale has explained her.

In the beautiful historic cemetery at Frankfort, not far from the graves of Daniel and Rebecca Boone, is another mystery grave. This one has a tapering and rather impressive old shaft, with no word of any sort cut on it. The story goes that in the dead of night the cemetery caretaker was awakened, bribed most lavishly to open the iron gates and go back to bed. When morning came a grave had been dug, a burial completed, the monument set in place. So far as we know this is exactly all that has ever been found out, though the guesswork has covered an exciting range.

And then there was the Lady in Black, a familiar figure of Victorian days in Louisville. Instead of pining in secret, she followed her faithless lover everywhere he went, arranging in her will for a substitute to wear the same black dress and mourning veil and to continue the "haunting" should she die before her "beloved."

Kentucky has her ghost stories, of course, a well-known one being that of the Gray Lady of Liberty Hall, now a historic shrine in Frankfort, once the attractive Dominion Georgian house of John Brown.

The last member of the family to live in the house often spoke of seeing the romantic, unhappy ghost—a bride, beautiful in filmy gray, weeping forever through the quiet house. She had been a visitor at Liberty Hall, where the sad news of her young husband's death in a runaway was brought to her—or so the story went.

Swift's Silver

A ghost, too, is said to have lived in John Swift's famous Cave of Silver, near the head of the Kentucky, since 1800, when Swift died. The treasure hunters who have combed that part of the country again and again would probably have risked a good deal of supernatural companionship if only they could have found that fabulous cave where the ghost *and* a rich silver lode, or great amounts of silver coin and bullion, have long been believed to be located.

The story of Swift's Silver is a true Treasure Island plot. There are varying versions, the general gist being that a George Munday followed a bear into a cave in 1740 and found a rich vein of silver ore. He was soon captured by Indians, who knew all about it, and for a few years he helped them mine silver. Later when he escaped, the English sailor, Swift, befriended him and was told the secret of the silver.

In 1761, Swift and a party of Spanish miners are supposed to have dug great amounts of the ore in this cave. Since he had no way of getting it out of the rough mountain country, he made a map, left the country, and planned to return. He is supposed never to have been able to locate it again, but he left his maps and records when he died, and ever since, periodic treasure hunts have been carried out. Some rumors have it that he was a counterfeiter, others that the silver was under a curse. Geologists generally doubt the existence of a big silver lode in Kentucky. But, after all, lode or cache, the legend of Swift's Silver is still very much alive.

In case our world were to be wiped out by atomic war, and some future survivor stumbled (in some cataclysmic way) on the Fort Knox gold reserve and then couldn't find it when he went back, new forty-niners—if there were enough people— would surely have a try at locating Kentucky's fabulous gold deposits, wouldn't they?

Wonders Never Cease

Certain early Kentucky surgeons were, indeed, miracle men. Without the help of modern equipment or anesthetics their achievements are amazing and they were regarded with respect and awe.

In 1806 Dr. Brashear of Bardstown took off at the hip joint the thigh of a mulatto boy who lived for many years afterward. It was the first time this operation had ever been attempted in America.

Three years later Dr. Ephraim McDowell of Danville removed a large ovarian tumor from Mrs. Jane Todd Crawford—the first case in the world of such surgery—and successful, too!

A couple of years after this there came a year which was to be christened Annus Mirabilis, for it was filled with wonders. It was at this time that the first steamboat came churning down the Ohio and stopped at the port of Louisville, terrifying its citizens and sending them to their knees for Providential aid.

Many people were sure a comet had fallen into the river, and that Judgment Day was at hand. Even when they were assured that it was a man-made wonder, it was regarded with much uneasiness.

The boat was the *New Orleans* (or *Orleans*), owned and piloted by Nicholas Roosevelt. After a good deal of difficulty it managed to negotiate the treacherous Falls of the Ohio, and continued its journey, the first steamer to ply the great inland rivers.

It was during this year of 1811 that great earthquake shocks and tremors were felt all over the state. This upheaval created Reelfoot Lake, a wild and unusual swamp lake in north Tennessee and southwestern Kentucky. And, in the midst of such disturbing phenomena as steam and earthquakes, came tales that the British were threatening America again.

"Again to the Battle..."

"Captains, awake!" ... Isaac Shelby had retired from public life and built Traveller's Rest, one of Kentucky's first stone houses. Here he was living as a prosperous farmer and mule breeder when again he heard the sound of gunfire and stepped forward to shoulder a rifle at the age of sixty-two, leading a force of volunteers in a march toward Detroit, and taking active part in the Battle of the Thames, in October, 1813.

It was in this battle that Colonel Richard M. Johnson of Kentucky was generally credited with killing the great Tecumseh, cutting much ground from under the feet of the Indians who had firmly believed their chief to be supernatural.

Earlier, General William Henry Harrison had won the Battle of Tippecanoe against the Shawnee Prophet, half-brother of Tecumseh, and the rumor had spread that the British would rally the Indians and threaten the Ohio Valley.

The Kentuckians had oversubscribed their quota for the War of 1812 against their old enemies, yet, when word came that Andy Jackson, down New Orleans way, needed help in the expected attack from the British there, a large force was hastily despatched.

The story goes that when these men reached Louisiana, they were in many cases without guns, having left them at the Thames, possibly. When Old Hickory heard of the situation, he stated flatly: "I don't believe it. I have never seen a Kentuckian without a gun, a bottle of whisky, and a pack of cards in my life!"

The Battle of New Orleans was, of course, disastrous to

Pakenham's Redcoats, who had to march across open ground while the sharpshooters of Kentucky (guns evidently having been provided) picked them off.

One young English officer wrote a touching account of the chill horror of marching, rank by rank, while a man fell with each ping of a rifle bullet. He mentioned one big sniper in a far-off tree, a great long-range marksman, even in his day, for "as regularly as he raised his rifle and pulled the trigger, a Redcoat fell." The Englishmen became fascinated with dread, wondering which of them would be the next sure target.

The famous song of Samuel Woodworth, "The Hunters of Kentucky," in a sense immortalized the battle and was an extremely popular number at any entertainment in the state for many a year:

> "... *the ground was dark and mucky.*
> *There stood John Bull in martial pomp*
> *But here stood old Kentucky!*
> *Oh Kentucky, the hunters of Kentucky!*
> *The hunters of—Kentucky!"*

Because of tragically slow communications this bloody battle had been fought two weeks after the war ended, the Treaty of Ghent having been negotiated on Christmas Eve, 1814, although it was not ratified until the following February 17. In the parleys Henry Clay is credited with brilliant diplomacy—or certainly the ability to bluff the British delegation in Europe as coolly as he often did his opponents in Lexington poker games—for he secured excellent terms for the United States, and again a war was over.

Actually it had been Clay's bold voice, as Speaker of the House in Congress, that had urged the beginning of the War of 1812 and a showdown of strength with John Bull. He was thirty-four years old, and already a lawyer, statesman, and orator of great national influence. At twenty he had been admitted to the bar. Leaving Richmond, Virginia, he moved to Lexington, and at twenty-two was a member of the convention entrusted with the revising of Kentucky's constitution.

It was his persuasive oratory and sound thinking that stopped a highly prejudiced legislature from banning the citing of English law as authority for court decisions in the state. As Carl Schurz reminds us, "He saved for Kentucky the treasures of English jurisprudence."

His eloquence was so telling that nobody defended by him was ever convicted. But he disliked to practice criminal law and stopped, once remarking, "I fear I have saved too many who ought to be hanged."

Among the causes Clay stood for with conviction were recognition of the South American republics, the Missouri Compromise, a moderate protective tariff, a regulated "retirement" of slavery, internal improvements of the country, and, above all, national unity and strength. His resolutions (the Compromise of 1850) delayed the Civil War ten years.

In his "fighting" career, he took part in several duels, the most famous being the one with John Randolph, after a diatribe from Randolph suggesting that Clay's appointment as President John Quincy Adams's Secretary of State had been a deal. When neither man was wounded in the first exchange of shots, Randolph decided not to try a second round.

In spite of Clay's enormous popularity and great public service, he was edged out three times in presidential races, once in the nominations by John Quincy Adams, twice in elections by Jackson and Polk respectively. His last chance was lost in 1848, when the Whigs nominated Zachary Taylor, hero of Buena Vista.

After Clay's first great national service—his key part in implementing and concluding the War of 1812—there was peace in the land. Again and again the silken tassels of Kentucky's corn turned golden under her blue summer skies. Business prospered and men laid the foundations of sizable fortunes, but among the few whose luck was on the downgrade was the aging hero George Rogers Clark whose partial paralysis resulted in a fall in which one of his legs was so badly burned that it had to be amputated. His old soldiers marched around his house during the operation banging on their drums and piping their fifes in an effort to distract him from the agony of the pain. While his fingers beat out the martial airs, his steady gray eyes watched every movement of the surgeon's hands.

General Lafayette, another idol of past days, visited the Kentucky scene and was lavishly entertained. "Society" flourished, and for a generation the Great Meadow was very lushly "in the bloom."

Louisville, which boasted more than seven hundred buildings, was declared a city, given a Council of Ten, and divided into five wards where politicking went on with true fervor. The canal was opened and the steamer *Uncas* squeezed through before a cheering crowd, overtopped by the local giant, Big Jim Porter, whose elegant hack was a favorite conveyance to guests patronizing the newly erected Galt House.

And then again, breaking this era of peace and prosperity, the bugle call was heard when on May 13, 1846, Congress proclaimed the existence of a state of war against the Republic of Mexico.

Kentucky was asked for thirty companies but organized more than a hundred. A fifth of General Zachary Taylor's rank and file were from his home state, and many of them, including Henry Clay, Jr., laid down their lives at the Battle of Buena Vista, a dearly bought American triumph.

It was, perhaps, the popularity attendant on this victory that led to Taylor's election as Kentucky's first president of the United States.

Fighting beside Taylor in Mexico was William Orlando Butler, who later served as one of the Peace Commissioners. He, like the other famous "Fighting Butlers" of his family, was an intrepid soldier and, rather surprisingly, an excellent poet, being the author of a nostalgic river song which still holds great appeal:

> *"O, Boatman, wind that horn again!*
> *For never did the listening air*
> *Upon its lambent bosom bear*
> *So wild, so soft, so sweet a strain!*
> *What though thy notes are sad and few,*
> *By every simple boatman blown,*
> *Yet is each pulse to nature true,*
> *And melody in every tone.*
> *How oft in boyhood's joyous day,*
> *Unmindful of the lapsing hours,*
> *I've loitered on my homeward way*
> *By wild Ohio's bank of flowers,*
> *While some lone boatman from the deck*
> *Poured his soft numbers to that tide,*
> *As if to charm from storm and wreck*
> *The boat where all his fortunes ride!..."*

CHAPTER 9

Steamboat Round the Bend

THE BEAUTIFUL OHIO, like a fickle woman, brought happiness and fortune to some of her lovers. Others she fired with ambition and led to despair and destruction.

There is a grave marked with the first iron tablet cast west of the Alleghenies whose legend reads: "Jacob Yoder was born at Reading, Pennsylvania, August 11, 1758; and was a soldier of the Revolutionary army in 1777 and 1778. He emigrated to the West in 1780; and in May 1782, from Fort Redstone, on the Monongahela River, in the First Flat Boat, that ever descended the Mississippi River, he landed in New Orleans, with a cargo of produce. He died April 7th, 1832, at his farm in Spencer County, Kentucky, and lies here interred beneath this tablet."

Poor John Fitch

Captain Yoder's friend, Connecticut-born John Fitch, had no such luck, no such stability, either, though he was unquestionably a genius. The two could talk together in German or Dutch, according to the report of one of the Yoder slaves, a man named Harry who had originally been brought into the country by Squire Boone. Fitch is described as being a short, stout man bustling with energy and full of ideas. By trade he was a clockmaker and a gunsmith, a sutler to the Revolutionary Army. After the war he took his depreciated Continental money and pre-empted a thousand acres of Kentucky land, acting as surveyor for himself and others. He was captured by the Indians and lived with them for a year before he was ransomed.

In 1780, while he was sitting on the bank of the Ohio, "the thought forced itself upon him that a good God had not provided such a magnificent stream without designing it for the use of his creatures, and that such use involved the overcoming its currents by a new mode of navigation."

He knew that, in England, Watt was propelling mills by steam and decided that this same power could be used to propel boats. He also considered the invention of a steam carriage but decided that this would not be practical. Within five years he built models of the boat and boiler which he presented to the American Philosophical Society. Within the next few years he built several full-scale boats, the first with side wheels and later ones with paddles, some making the passage between Philadelphia and Burlington, a distance of twenty miles, at a speed of seven and one-half miles an hour.

When their boilers burst he could not find money enough to replace them and became discouraged. He wrote three volumes of manuscript which he sealed and sent to the Philadelphia Library with the request that they be opened thirty years after his death. They contained his speculations on mechanics and the story of his bitter disappointments.

"The day will come," he wrote, "when some powerful man will get fame and riches from my invention; but nobody will believe that poor John Fitch can do anything worthy of attention." This statement was later proved to be true, for the boats successfully built by Fulton and Livingston after Fitch's death employed the same principles.

Fitch, as well as Fulton, had tried to get help from England and France and Spain but was unsuccessful in these attempts and retired to his Kentucky lands in despair, seeking relief in "habitual intoxication." Soon he lost all of his holdings except three hundred acres and he bargained to give half of this land to a tavern keeper if he would take care of him as long as he lived and give him a pint of whisky a day; later he gave the man more land for an increase in liquor.

Much of the time he brooded upon the controversy he had had with James Rumsey, a Virginian who emigrated to Kentucky. The two men without knowing each other had made models of steamboats and showed them to General Washington. Fitch claimed that when he met Rumsey he told him of his plans and that Rumsey had taken advantage of him. Some years later, when Robert Fulton brought a suit seeking to prove that he was the inventor of steam navigation, he lost his case when a pamphlet was produced proving that both Fitch and Rumsey had prior claims. The point was even made that Fitch's specifications, deposited with the American consul in France, had been entrusted for a time to Fulton.

Whatever the actual rights and wrongs may have been, in the end it was Fulton who achieved the fame and fortune. Other men besides Fitch and Rumsey broke their hearts on the steamboat's wheel. Edward West of Lexington made several working models, but could never get the necessary backing for full-scale production. West did make one big practical contribution to the country, and a much-needed one. He perfected a method of making strong, sharp, cheap, plentiful nails.

And poor John Fitch? At fifty-five, thoroughly discouraged, he took his own life, there in Bardstown, bequeathing to one friend his spectacles, walking stick, beaver hat, and shoe buckles, and to another the remainder of his estate, which proved to be of even less value.

Water Highway

But the enormous value of steamboats—anybody's steamboats —was now known to be immeasurable. Boatbuilding soon became an obsession, and all along both sides of the Ohio ships were constructed and launched, not only for river use, but for salt water, too, a few being piloted through the Gulf and up the seaboard with the hope of selling them for ocean travel.

Kentucky's Captain Henry M. Shreve had made news in the late autumn of 1814 by taking his steamer *Enterprise* down to New Orleans to help Andy Jackson. And it was again Captain Shreve who made everybody take very real notice when he designed his new boat, the *G. Washington,* with a shallow draft and flat bottom, so much better suited to easy loading and safer navigation on the changeable rivers.

Kentucky grew with the steamboat even faster than with the busy old flatboat. She grew in actual geographical size, too, for Andrew Jackson, a few years after the Battle of New Orleans, made a treaty with the Chickasaw, gaining for Tennessee and Kentucky 4,600 square miles of new western territory—the Jackson Purchase—extending Kentucky Country to the Ohio confluence and a short stretch of the mighty Mississippi.

There was some concern that Robert Fulton, whose prestige was enormous after the *Clermont's* sensational maiden voyage on the Hudson in 1807, and his partner Livingston would be able to enforce the monopoly patent they held for the use of steam power on the country's arterial rivers. But the New West ignored it and the hammers of the boatbuilders and the rush of steam, the scream of whistles, and the thrashing of paddle wheels resounded all up and down the waterfronts of the Ohio.

When the Portland Canal at Louisville was finally finished in 1830, and the hazard of the Falls removed, the old broadhorns and awkward rafts of yesterday were almost entirely replaced by steamboats, there being nearly seven hundred of them on the Mississippi, Ohio, and connecting rivers within four or five years.

The steamboats plied the waters of some of the tributary streams, especially the Kentucky River, where locks were built at necessary points, but it was, of course, the Ohio that was second only to the Mississippi as chief water highway of this new era of steam.

Floating Palaces

There still remained the natural perils of snag, planter, and sawyer, of sand bar and shifting channel, and these took heavy toll of the new queens. The difficulty of easing a steamboat over shoals in low-water times was acute and the danger of fire was omnipresent, especially when undue speed was applied, which was often the case.

The temptation to race the beauties was completely irresistible to the lordly captains. To show their prowess and settle bets, challenges were made and met every week. The pressure of too much steam often meant a burst boiler and a flaming catastrophe, with a horrifying number of deaths and enormous loss of property, but still the races went on.

The boasts of the bewhiskered Beau Brummels of the river echoed in essence the "cock-a-doodle-doos" of the old keelboat bullies. "I can take my girl right across country in a heavy dew!" "I am willing to accept any wager, gentlemen, that this *Belle of Paducah* or any other packet of our company will leave your tub thrashing the bottom like a catfish caught in the backwater."

These contests drew great crowds along the shores and gave Currier and Ives the inspiration for the pictures that decorated almost every Kentucky cabin and mansion. From spur-of-the-moment affairs, with emergency fueling in the shape of slabs of bacon, to widely heralded occasions such as the famous *Robert E. Lee—Natchez* high drama near the close of the era (sung not only on the Mississippi and Ohio, but all over the continent), they were sporting events of truly titanic proportions.

Social life on the river boats in the middle 1800's was luxurious and varied. The gambling gentry was, of course, greatly in evidence, and the flamboyance of their jewelry and haberdashery dazzled the eyes of country people and even those of more sophisticated city folks who thronged the velvet-carpeted saloons and crowded the damask-covered tables to enjoy the twelve-course dinners and beefsteak breakfasts served with such punctilious ceremony.

The cry of "Steamboat 'round the bend" never failed to raise a crowd on the cobblestone quays which lined the Ohio. The visit of one of the fabulous floating palaces was a never-to-be-forgotten occurrence. Enormous, white, and majestic as a summer cloud, lit by night with thousands of candles in gilt and crystal chandeliers, mirrored and frescoed, exquisitely "appointed," these Queens of the Western Waterways had a luxury appeal that was potent, and their business was immense.

Among their patrons were planters and their families from the Deep South, for Kentucky was something of a summer resort. Within her borders there were numerous popular springs, where "fancified" frame hotels with their flocks of family cottages offered lavish hospitality and opportunities for romance and marriage. The gentlemen arrived with tall beaver hats and gold-headed canes, and the young ladies with half a dozen Saratoga trunks crammed with crinoline petticoats and lavender-scented satin ball gowns.

Even Louisville got her share of these vacationers, for the Galt House and the Louisville Hotel offered comforts that could not be surpassed. Their verandas were lined with rows of upholstered rocking chairs, and the dim-lit parlors provided many a cozy-corner loveseat. There were fireworks, dazzling bursts of glory falling like comets from the sky, to be extinguished in an instant as they dropped into the water down there below the Galt House balcony. There were strawberry suppers and singing parties in the porticoed homes of friends all up and down Walnut and Chestnut Streets and way out in the almost-country of Broadway. And there were promenades for those whose churches frowned upon the sin of dancing. This ban could sometimes be skirted by calling such an affair a play-party rather than a hop and introducing games such as "Skip-to-My-Lou-My-Darling" rather than worldly polkas and frivolous lancers.

Hotel guests occupied spare moments variously. A gentleman could usually find an interesting card game or cockfight if he were so inclined. A lady was endowed with every luxury of service. Each young miss had her attendant cicerone and was often also accompanied by a small Negro boy, genially termed her "chocolate drop." It was his responsibility to carry scented notes for her, retrieve her mitts or lacy handkerchief, or stir up a breeze with his long-handled peacock-feather fan.

After shopping, a siesta, and a sunset interlude of gossip or flirtation in those cushioned veranda rockers, our heroines were ready for the late table d'hôte dinner (fifty cents per person). This included a choice of eighteen meats—pigeon pie, saddle of mutton, arcade of pheasants, and so on—fifteen vegetables, five hot breads, and at least thirty desserts. The number of items served any guest was not restricted, and if she (or more probably he, the eighteen-inch waistline being a prime concern of most females of the day) wished, she was at liberty to order everything on the menu.

Louisville was a popular summer resort for the Mississippi River gamblers for some several years, and some elaborate gambling boats were familiars here. When a city ordinance forbade their tying up at the quay, their proprietors simply anchored them at midstream, offering discreet skiff service to the customers.

Regular steamboat passenger service on the Ohio and the Kentucky flourished proudly, except for the Civil War years, until the last years of the nineteenth century. Today only the *Delta Queen* books passenger trips on the Ohio and Mississippi via Louisville. Occasional showboats and small excursion paddle wheelers for pleasure trips ply a limited trade. On the Kentucky, barge parties, once legion, are rare now. Gliding over a dance floor that gives to the rhythm of the orchestra and dancers while the barge sails effortlessly (thanks to a stout little tugboat's pushing) is an experience to appreciate and a memory to treasure, for the backdrop of the majestic gray rock palisades of the Kentucky River is beautiful beyond description, the one unchanging facet in the rapidly changing scene of the river picture.

The Ohio is still, perhaps contrary to general belief, a transportation giant. Her traffic has more than doubled in the past ten years. Some of her immense radar-controlled tow barges would cover two and a half acres of ground and she is said to move more freight than the Panama Canal.

When these monstrous plateaux glide by during the darkness of the night they seem to be the ghosts of Corn Island and all those others which were submerged beneath the waves a hundred years ago. Was that shrill little peep the call of a drowsy waterfowl or was it the far-off sound of a fife piped by some buckskin lad to summon his companions, faithful followers all of them of that redheaded giant and hero, George Rogers Clark? "Kaskaskia, Kaskaskia!" The sound grows dim—dimmer, only the waves of the Ohio whisper the music now, lapping the shore as the barge recedes into the mystery of darkness, darkness of place—and of time.

CHAPTER 10

"The Day Goes by Like a Shadow O'er the Heart"

OLD KENTUCKY COUNTRY was split wide-open on the tragic question of slavery, long before the War Between the States. Slavery was protected by law, and well protected, for most of the lawmakers were determined slaveholders. A number of leaders were anti-slavery in principle, however, and some of them freed their own slaves. The ministers of most of the churches inveighed against slavery, so much so that a regulation was made, for a time, barring any man of the cloth from holding public office.

Economists—some of them—argued that Kentucky was in no wise dependent on slave labor for her farm work, as were the plantation states of the South. The slave trader, by whom many Negroes were sold down the river, was looked on with contempt and revulsion, but he flourished, sometimes on the sly, sometimes openly with newspaper advertising. Large "jails" existed where slaves were bought up and held for shipment to market.

Among statesmen declaring themselves, eventually, against slavery were Henry Clay, Cassius M. Clay (always strongly anti), Robert J. Breckinridge, United States Senator J. R.

Underwood, and John G. Fee. The American Colonization Society was formed of both the antis and the pros, to deport Kentucky Negroes to a "Kentucky in Liberia" in Africa. This was expensive and the tropical climate a health hazard to the Negroes who did go, so the plan fell far short of its objective.

Many a slaveholder felt the practice of slavery morally wrong, while many a man who had never owned a slave resented Northern "railroaders" so hotly that they sided with the pro-slavery faction on the grounds that Kentucky's "Constitutional Rights" were in danger.

A number of plans for "orderly emancipation" were discussed, but pressure from the pro-slavery groups, and indecision and doubt as to what to do in Abolition groups, made a stalemate.

Generally speaking, Kentucky's race relations have over the years been exceptionally good, because men of good will of both races have tried hard to make and keep them so. A story came to us very recently that illustrates one attitude we can all be proud of. A colored man who is headwaiter in a popular restaurant in Louisville is a most pleasant and efficient person, well liked by all his customers. When news came that his son had received a West Point appointment, everyone hurried to congratulate him. In one of these conversations, in answer to the question, "How does your son feel about it? Excited?" he said:

"And a little bit scared—he told me that. And I just told him, 'So are all the other boys. This is a big thing for any young fellow. And before you feel sorry for yourself about any little thing you might not be crazy about, just remember *all* those new boys have adjustments to make, too. You're just like all of them when it comes to that.' "

Brother Against Brother

Kentucky tried to stay neutral as the fratricidal War Between the States developed, a completely unrealistic attitude but an understandable one, since her differences of opinion were so deep-seated that unified action was out of the question.

The bare idea of leaving the Union, in which there was now such sound strength and stability, was unwise and reprehensible in the eyes of many conscientious Kentucky people. Just as unthinkable to others was to stay within an organization that trampled State Rights and interfered with private concerns in highhanded and unreasonable arbitrariness.

In many towns the same parade grounds were used in turn by the Home Guard and the State Guard, one Union, one Rebel in sympathy. Prayers were offered for the quick victory of "our just cause," often in the same church service, but with bitter differences in the hearts of suppliants. An unprejudiced jury was impossible to panel when the politics of the opponents in a court trial were known. Banks and businesses refused credit to customers of the "wrong" persuasion. The isolationist Know-Nothing party kept its head in the sand, when it wasn't stirring up riots or haranguing the realistic. Tempers flared, and friendships and family ties were broken.

And when war did come, its most agonizing implications came home to the border country. Many and many a time, brothers of opposite beliefs prayed nightly not to meet the other in actual fighting. Many a personal story has been handed down in its intimate particulars to each generation of listeners.

"As I told you, these were really all neighborhood boys, some of them with John Hunt Morgan's men, and some of them in that Yankee platoon trying to catch them. I remember standing —I was a little girl—in our front hall. Mamma was crying, and something kept rattling against the glass panes at either side of our door. They said it was grape shot. Your Great-uncle Johnse was killed on our own front steps. He was just sixteen. He— tried to get to the house, and Pappa ran to help him. . . . Pappa was at home because he'd been wounded and was getting well. No, it wasn't a battle, goodness no! There never was but the one real battle—the Battle of Perryville—to take place on Kentucky soil in the War Between the States.

"Maybe you'd call the trouble out at Grandfather's farm that morning a skirmish—there were a lot of raids and skirmishes— and it wasn't important enough to go in a history book . . . but Brother Johnse was killed, and so were the Tavner boys, and everybody's horses and stock were driven off, everybody's in the whole Grier's Creek neighborhood, and two of our cousins' houses were burned. . . . That was a pity, too, because your Cousin Sarah's was so pretty. Big brick house, built about two years before Kentucky was a state—that was 1792 of course—and it had those high narrow windows to keep Indians from shoot- ing in, or peeking in. . . .

"Pappa—my father, your great-great-grandfather—was born in that house, in that big black-walnut bed that's in my bed- room now. He saved some of Cousin Sarah's things, you see, though they weren't speaking after her husband joined the Union Army and broke his word to Pappa when he did. But of course all of us went to help when we saw that smoke rising from Cousin Sarah's place. We drove over in a spring wagon, all of us, Mamma and the girls and me, and the colored people, except Aunt Mincy who was lame. Pappa had ridden on ahead . . . oh, we still had the horses then. Don't you remember? They didn't get the horses till next day, early in the dawn. I *told* you that . . . well, maybe I did exaggerate a little, because we had a mule left, and some pigs and a heifer, when the raid next day was over.

"I'll never forget Cousin Sarah. She was standing there watching her house burn. Pappa came out of the door with a great big gold-framed portrait and tilted it against a tree. Cousin Sarah said, 'Good afternoon, Matilda'—that was Mamma, of course—'this is an unexpected honor. Will you tell Mr. Johnse' —that was Pappa—'that I hope he's satisfied?'

"And Pappa told us children and the colored people to get out the silver and what else we could, but nobody except him was to go upstairs where the fire had broken through the roof. He said, 'Matilda, tell this pitiable cousin of mine that if that fool Abolitionist she married had had enough brains to wad a shotgun, he would have left some protection for her, and perhaps this wouldn't have happened.'

"We got out a good many things, things that had been pretty, but, pretty or not, furniture and covers and all look so terrible dropped helter-skelter in a front yard. . . . Cousin Sarah didn't know about Brother Johnse till she came home with us to stay for a while. I reckon she was in a state of shock, as people say now. But she wouldn't say she was sorry about Brother Johnse, though he'd always been her favorite. She lived with us—her husband died at Vicksburg—till she died years later, but she and Pappa never did speak. It was always, 'Matilda, tell Mr. Johnse this,' and 'Tillie, remind your Cousin Sarah that'— it got to be *your* cousin, though she was Pappa's cousin—

". . . and then our colored people left, too, all but Aunt Mincy. I suppose we did have a hard 'make' of it, but I was young, and we had some good times. . . . But I've always held that all of us worked harder before Emancipation than afterward. It was a matter of pride, and there were strict laws in Kentucky, too, as to shelter and clothing a man had to provide his slaves. Every one of us girls—and I was little, right about eight years old, when I learned to knit—had to knit a sock for our 'people' every day of the world except Christmas and the Sabbath, before we had time to ourselves. . . .

"Oh, we could get cloth and some few made-up things when the steamboats came up the Kentucky from the Ohio, but right up to my time a lot of carding and spinning and weaving was done in a big weaving room at the end of a dog-trot to one side of the house. We dyed the cloth or the yarn, too, with madder and indigo and walnut bark and peach leaves. I remember it well. We had to take swamp-root tonic, and sassafras brew to keep off ague and thin the blood in the spring.

"We were country people, remember, and though we did drive to town two or three times a week, we depended on ourselves and on each other for a lot of things. Pappa had a sawmill down at the bottom of the hill from the house, maybe a quarter of a mile from the ferry. He always kept a man there to run logs through the water-powered ripsaw for anybody who hauled them or maybe floated them to the mill.

"The Moores had a flour mill—and cornmeal could be ground there, too, a few miles up the creek. And everybody killed their own meat, and brewed homemade wine, and saved out a little tobacco for the men smokers—and I'm ashamed to say sometimes chewers—and canned and preserved and pickled —I started to say 'enough for an army' but that's a foolish thing to say, once you know what one little neighborhood squad can do to a farm. . . ."

Poison Pens

Anthologies such as *The Civil War in Song and Story* (1870) have preserved some choice literary flights.

Feelings were fanned by partisan writings, absurd to read now, but extremely inflammatory at the time. Governor Beriah Magoffin, known to be pro-Southern, was the subject of a poem

in an Indiana paper, "The Meeting on the Border," apropos of
one of his many efforts to preserve Kentucky's neutrality:

"The Civil War had just begun
And caused much consternation,
While O. P. Morton governed one
Great State of this Great Nation—So he did!

Magoffin governed old Kentuck
And Dennison Ohio;
And no three humans had more pluck
Than this puissant trio—So they hadn't!

Magoffin was the leading man,
He telegraphed to Perry,
And writ by post to Dennison
To meet him in a hurry—So he did!

And Dennison and Morton too
Believed they had good reason
To fear Magoffin sought to do
Some act of hellish treason—So they did!

But they concluded it was best
To do as he demanded,
So they would have a chance to test
The question: "Is he candid?"—So they did!

Magoffin 4 A.M. did fix
By post and by the wire,
But when the hour had come—why nix
Come raus was he—Beriah—So he was!

And then you could have heard them swear,
Them chaps along with Perry
They cussed and stamped and pulled the air
For they were angry, very—So they were!

And now if they could mix his "todd"
They'd put some pizen stuff in
And serve their country and their God
By killing off "Meguffin"—SO THEY WOULD!"

General Morgan was also attacked in verse:

Kentucky, Oh Kentucky!

"John Morgan's foot is on thy shore, Kentucky Oh
  Kentucky!
His hand is on thy stable door, Kentucky Oh Kentucky!
You'll see your good gray mare no more
He'll ride her till her back is sore
And leave her at some stranger's door, Kentucky, Oh
  Kentucky!

For feeding John you're paying dear, Kentucky Oh
  Kentucky!
His very name now makes you fear, Kentucky Oh
  Kentucky!
In every valley far and near
He's gobbled every horse and steer
You'll rue his raids for many a year, Kentucky, Oh
  Kentucky!

Yet you have many a traitorous fool, Kentucky, Oh
  Kentucky!
Who still will be the rebel's tool, Kentucky Oh Kentucky!
They'll learn to yield to Abra'm's rule
In none but Johnny's costly school
At cost of every animule, Kentucky Oh Kentucky!"

A return sally goes:

> *"Jeff Davis rides a white horse,*
>   *Lincoln rides a mule.*
> *Jeff Davis is a gentleman,*
>   *And Lincoln is a fule."*

A squad of Indiana volunteers in the Kentucky mountains
once questioned an old woman in a cabin.

"Are you a secesh, old lady?"

"No."

"Union, then?"

"No."

"Just what are you?"

"A Baptist. Allus have been. What're you?"

Quite an account of two remarkably daring Southern girls appeared in a little Kentucky paper. "Miss Diana Smith of Jackson, . . . a beautiful girl and also a member of the Methodist Episcopal Church, has always been regarded as pious and exemplary. She is descended from a race of unflinching nerve, and satisfied with nothing less than freedom as unrestrained as the pure air of her mountain home.

"Although a tender and delicate flower upon whose cheek the bloom of sixteen summers still lingers, she has been five times captured by the Yankees, and marched in *manacles,* a prisoner. . . . She was never released but, in each instance of capture, made her escape. She too has seen service in several battles in which her father engaged the enemy. . . . Her trusty rifle has made more than one vile Yankee bite the dust.

"In a recent trip through enemy lines she was accompanied by Miss Duskie, also a heroine. On one occasion this fearless girl, surrounded by fifty Yankees and Union men, rushed through their ranks with a daring that struck terror to their craven hearts. . . . The great crime with which these ladies are charged by the enemy, is cooking, washing, mending, and buying powder for our soldiers."

"Politics the Damnedest"

Though Kentucky did not officially secede, and actually sent more Union than Confederate soldiers into the fighting, she was badly treated by the government when the war ended. Great bitterness resulted, and the growing feeling that had Lincoln lived things would surely have been different became a conviction with the passage of time.

Harsh government regulations, plus guerrilla warfare that continued long after Appomattox, made Kentuckians suspicious and fearful of one another. Nobody knew whom to trust, as old personal grudges were often paid off slyly by those with Yankee influence. The tendency to draw together in familiar groups—after all, everybody knew their home folks, whether or not they had agreed in the Late Conflict—made for factionalism.

The excellent recent *History of Kentucky* by Thomas D. Clark of Lexington blames the oppression of Kentucky by government authorities for the fiercely partisan sectional differences which have beset state politics ever since. Certainly the most violent example of factional feuding was the controversial Goebel Affair in 1900.

Briefly, and sketchily: William Goebel, Democratic candidate for governor, was defeated by William Taylor, western Kentucky Republican. The fight was bitter and fraud was immediately charged by both sides, threats made, and tempers lost. The eastern mountain counties, strongly Republican, were furious when the Democrats who controlled the legislature demanded a committee to work with it in investigating the election and possibly throwing the Republicans out of the Statehouse.

Frankfort was a powder keg and matches were handy. Mountaineers armed with guns walked the streets, and crowds of angry voters on both sides thronged the town. On the grounds of the Statehouse, where discussions of the touch-and-go situation were under way, Goebel was shot from a window of the office building next door. He was sworn in as governor at the Capitol Hotel, where he was carried, wounded, the special committee having decided in favor of the Democrats. Goebel died four days later, though the bitterness created by the whole situation lived for many, many years.

The seal of Kentucky presents two gentlemen shaking hands, with the motto, "United We Stand, Divided We Fall." And Kentuckians are intensely loyal to their state, but their viewpoint is intensely personal, too, and to many of them Kentucky means, "*My* neighborhood, *my* hometown, *my* county."

This is a natural situation when we read that, a hundred years after Kentucky became a state, there were almost 2,000,000 people living here, *all native-born* American Kentuckians except for fewer than 100,000. The 1950 census showed the population approaching 3,000,000, the percentage of natives still being unusually high.

Foreigners have of course come to Kentucky, but never in great waves as they did in the late nineteenth century to the large Northern cities. One can stand on any street corner in Kentucky all day long without hearing any language except English—oh, well, any language except *American,* we'd better say. It is, however, often said that much Kentucky speech tends toward an accentless median. It may be accentless sometimes, but it can be mighty florid any time!

From the excellent *Courier-Journal Sunday Magazine* "Story of Kentucky," the work of many contributors, published in several issues in 1942, comes as colorful an effusion as we've ever read or heard. It was told by the late Governor W. O. Bradley about Representative Mullins, who went to the Frankfort legislature in the early 1870's on the fine old Kentucky River packet, *Blue Wing.*

" 'Feller citizens,' he addressed the court-day crowds when he came home to report, 'when you elected me, I wisht I might cut the tallest pine ever growed in the mountings, strip the limbs from same and make it into an enormous pen, dipping it in the waters of the mighty Kentucky River, and write acrost yon clouds, "GOD BLESS THE PEOPLE OF ESTILL COUNTY!"

" 'When I went to Frankfort we wended our winding sinuosi-ties amidst labyrinthine meanderings, and the batlets and the owlets and the birdlets flew outen their hiding places to cry in a loud voice:

" ' "Sail on, Mullins, thou proud defender of thy country's liberties!"

" 'When I reached Frankfort I went to the Legislatur hall, and there I spied many purty perlicues a hangin' on the ceilin' for which you have been shamefully robbed of by unjust taxa-tion. When matters of small importance come before the body, I laid like a bull-pup a-baskin' in the sunshine with a blue-bottle fly ticklin' of my nose; but when matters of great im-portance come up, I riz from my seat like the Numidian Lion of the desert, shuck the dew-drops from my mane, and give three loud shrieks for liberty!' "

CHAPTER 11

Sunlight and Moonshine

"There's a Long, Long Trail A-winding"

THOUGH KENTUCKY has always been predominantly farming country, she is changing rapidly. Particularly since the great industrial expansion caused by World War II, new manufacturing concerns, giants of every specie, have moved into her cities and larger towns.

Tobacco and bourbon whisky have been big business here since the beginning of Kentucky time, and they still are. But in World War I days almost the only other products offered in amounts huge enough to dominate national statistics were baseball bats and minnow buckets.

Our Boys in Khaki, enforced visitors at Camp Taylor from 1917 to 1919, danced with Kentucky girls at Louisville's old Hawaiian Gardens (so named because of a row of potted palms), dashed around the country in motorcycle sidecars, paraded to "Over There" and "Keep the Home Fires Burning," and set off "across the pond." Returning for visits, later, they soon found nostalgic old Camp Taylor gone with the wind of factories and housing projects.

Many a G.I. of World War II was quartered at various Kentucky camps, too, the majority at Fort Knox, still an enormous

Armored Force center. And during these portentous years, Kentucky's minnow-bucket pre-eminence has widened to include near-records in such items as rocket fins, laminated ship timbers, electronic tubes, synthetic rubber, dishwashers, and blood-donor kits for her Red Cross Regional Blood Bank.

This industrial growth brings joy to many chambers of commerce, but some several of the small towns still lie low, hoping to be by-passed by big business. The farmers need the labor, already so costly, and can hardly meet the competition of soaring wages. The town-and-country life has been interdependent in so many Kentucky counties for so many generations that drastic change is frightening.

It is true that country people, tiring of farm responsibilities, have been moving to towns and cities over the years. But the love of the land is deeply inbred, and some of them keep possession of their farms. In turn, a good many city people tend to move to the country if they can manage it, but according to the old-timers this is only a sort of play-farming, for these country-living-city-working neophytes don't even object to daylight-saving time!

The cities adopt daylight-saving time each summer, but few truly rural districts will accept it, objecting strongly enough to keep the legislature from doing away with "God's time" as a state-wide measure.

Tourists are often confused by courthouse clocks that hop back and forth within a radius of a very few miles. A case in point appeared in a local paper recently. It seems that an out-of-state family found itself locked in the "Daniel Boone" Cemetery in Frankfort one late afternoon. An agile young son managed to scale a spiked fence and call the police, who couldn't let them out because the custodian, in charge of the only key to the iron gate, was absent from his usual haunts.

The weary father of the imprisoned family and his wearier

wife explained that they had set their watches in nearby Harrodsburg, so that *their* time was still within an hour of the evening deadline. The Law ferreted out a rusty back gate and, after denuding it of generations of honeysuckle, managed to force it open. In front of it there was a deep ditch which had to be filled with rocks before the travelers' car could make its exit. During the long delay the several children had been picnicking on tomorrow's lunch, which was packed in the car, "and," said our editor, "the spirit of Dan'l surely must have sighed as it recalled occasions when the old pioneer was lost without so much as a bottle of pop or a ham-on-rye to give him cheer. But he could tell time from the sun and stars."

The farmer's arguments against daylight-saving time seem abstruse to his city friends—something about milking cows and feeding chickens, and dew on the hay and the tobacco. One grizzled tenant-cropper clinched his point with a reporter from the city paper, "Just answer me this, young feller. Does they really *save* any time?"

Thanks to Sir Walter

Tobacco time is important, for this crop is of prime interest to the state's farm population, bringing in more than $200,-000,000 a year. The first White Burley seeds sold for five dollars a teaspoonful, and in early days the price of a good horse was twenty-six pounds of "weed."

Tobacco was acceptable legal tender in Virginia and Kentucky well into the nineteenth century, and has from the beginning been Kentucky's chief money crop. As a farm-wife summed it up wistfully, "The tobacco market has spoiled Christmas around here for years."

She didn't mean that prices were always bad—they're often

tiptop. But December is the anxious and all-important market month. Even when tobacco has survived such hazards as hail, rust, and house burn, the auction price is the last big river to cross. Many towns have markets, but Lexington, for loose-leaf Burley, is the world's largest, handling about 100,000,000 pounds a year. Wherever the warehouse "floor," the men with the wagons of weed, lined up to get in, are anxious indeed, for a year's income hangs in the balance.

Tobacco is, and always was, almost a twelve-month job, from seeding it and canvasing (February and March) the beds, transplanting to the field (specially fertilized and prepared) in June, cultivating, Paris-greening, suckering, to the cutting (in late August usually), housing, curing, stripping, and making into "hands," and finally hauling to the big warehouse "floors."

From the Bright Belt—the White Burley varieties raised chiefly in central Kentucky—to the Dark Tobacco of western Kentucky, it costs money to raise tobacco, money and muscle. To see the handsome plants, five feet or more tall, the giant leaves tapering to the top of the stalk and a spiky pink bloom (if it's allowed to go to seed), is a fine sight. To walk or ride horseback through a barn after cutting time and look up into folds of yellow-green velvet is an experience to remember.

The big barns—usually about seventy feet long, forty wide, and thirty-two high, each built to hold some five acres' yield— are set on bare knolls for sun and ventilation. The plants are hung in the barns on long sticks suspended from tiers—handhandled all the way. It takes a daring worker to start at the ridgepole, many sharing one opinion expressed in Virgil Steed's *Kentucky Tobacco Patch:* "I'll do *anything,* but I *won't* shinny tobacco up to the top of this here barn."

Violence has punctuated tobacco's history in Kentucky—the night riders of the early twentieth century having been particularly determined to force all the growers into the various

pools and equities by burning the full barns of the noncon-
formists.

Nowadays every grower's tobacco acreage is strictly rationed
by government regulation. This situation the independent sons
of the soil find highly irksome. They have seen only one
recourse, and this they exercise with such skill and resource that
the results are astonishing. The acreage may have shrunk, but
careful culture has managed to increase and almost double the
crop.

It is hard indeed for a farmer who has been brought up in
the shadow of the tobacco market to face the true facts. Rugged
individualist that he is by profession and inheritance, he can't
realize that what he does in his small way affects the tobacco
pool. He sees his neighbors increasing their yield and, by gum,
he can outraise them if he tries. He *knows* tobacco.

He can read the disturbing news that one third of year-
before-last's crop is still in the pool of the Burley Growers'
Co-operative Association. He reads about minimum price-
support payments made through the government's Commodity
Credit Corporation. He hears that the state now has about a
three-and-a-half-year supply of Burley on hand and a feeling
of panic and resentment assails him.

The experts are working hard to encourage a different approach to the raising of tobacco, and experiments are constantly
being made to show the way that "lower production per acre,
with increased attention to quality—low nicotine content and
fine leaf—can be equated into higher incomes per acre than
high yields from smaller allotments."

High Spirits

Bourbon whisky is another Kentucky money crop, regarded as a fine asset or hideous liability by various factions, who voice their opinions with characteristic energy.

Funk and Wagnall's *Standard Encyclopedia* defines the Gaelic word *uisgebeatha* as meaning water of life and the local variety —Bourbon—was named for the county which was one of the nine organized by the Virginia legislature before Kentucky became an independent state. It was "invented" there in 1789 by the Reverend Elijah Craig in Georgetown, now in Scott County, when "white mule" was first stored in charred oak barrels or kegs, making a mellower, tastier "sippage" of a deep amber hue.

At that time there were some two thousand stills already in existence, mostly private affairs, no more unusual than a smokehouse, the idea of a tax on corn whisky being thought outrageous.

But today's situation is quite a different affair.

Kentucky leads the nation in distilling bourbon whisky and the taxes derived from this industry go a long way toward the support of her schools. National public revenues from alcoholic beverages during the calendar year of 1955 amounted to $3,785,-058,733—a tidy sum, even in these days.

The related businesses are also of great economic importance. The white oak that is used for the barrels must be cut and sawed, coopered and bound with metal hoops, trucked and stored. The production of seals, foil, labels, corks, cartons, all offer jobs to thousands of workmen. Approximately four dollars per case of whisky goes for advertising and promotional work, and much of this is directed toward temperance, in that word's literal meaning of "habitual moderation," with the appeal of such slogans as, "When it's one for the road, make that one coffee!"

The exceedingly high taxes on whisky have long been a point of argument in Kentucky, the pros being willing and often determined to tax it out of existence if possible, the cons wailing that its tax burden is already preposterous.

One ingenious way in which a legal distiller met the competition between his taxed product and the cheaper moonshine that floods certain markets, and no tax about it, was to bottle and offer to the trade colorless, raw, new whisky labeled "Moonshine." We don't know how successful he was, but his premise was that, even though he couldn't meet the illegal price competition, he could put out a familiar-looking facsimile, and stress the point that it was as represented, and not the gruesome concoction sometimes palmed off by the "shiners" on bargainhunting customers.

From the Whisky Rebellion in Pennsylvania in 1794—with which a good many Kentuckians were in sympathy, though they never stirred one up at home—to the present day, personal rebellions against liquor taxes come to light in local and federal courts of the region with monotonous regularity.

Kentucky isn't alone as a favorite stamping ground for moonshiners, but from the Purchase to the eastern hills she has her full share. It was estimated that at the start of World War II there were easily one hundred illegal stills to every legal distillery here, and that out of 200,000,000 gallons made in one year, 40,000,000 were illicit, a case of "private enterprise come hell or high water."

The old argument, "A feller makes hoe cakes outen his corn, don't he? Why can't he cook up a job of red-eye?" has a certain justification, but the "revenooer" knows that little jug of redeye, little grains of corn, cost the state and the nation tremendous losses in taxes. He also knows that when the tough moonshiners go commercial in a big way, they are likely to use lye, wood alcohol, or anything else for "authority," with horrifying results to their customers.

There is however a lot of everyday drama performed in a strictly Kentucky accent in our federal courts here, for, as in any other "calling," there are moonshiners and moonshiners. Now and again a big ring or conspiracy of "barrel sweaters" is rounded up. (Barrels recently drained of bonded bourbon are bought up and steamed to coax about a gallon of "spirits" per barrel which had been absorbed by the wood.)

At other times the catch is small and personal.

"Shucks, I was just takin' a jug of 'vigors' to a sick ole man, an' they *jailed* me!"

"Me sellin' it? No, sir! I never sold a drap in my life, Jedge. I raffles it—two bits a chanst. Them whisky jugs they found down home was *door prizes*. I aimed to *give* 'em away! Nothin' wrong about that, now is they?"

The law reads that anybody working for an illegal stiller is as guilty as the owner and operator. "Why, I wasn't *workin'* fer nobody. They never ast me to! I was just out huntin' ginseng."

"At four o'clock in the morning? Kind of dark, wasn't it?"

"I can find 'seng in the dark."

"You found the still, all right!"

"Just stumbled on it, you might say. Took a little drink of beer."

(Beer is the local name of fermenting mash juice.)

"You were seen building up the fire at the still."

"Is that a fack? . . . well, I might have chunked it up some, if they ast me to. If you was out huntin' 'seng an' a feller says, 'Put that there log on my fire, Stranger,' wouldn't you kindly do it?"

"Would you have been so kind if you'd known an Alcohol Tax Evasion man was after you, and was watching you from the woods?"

"I reckon mabbe not. We never knowed he was up thar. We knowed he was stayin' in town—evvybody knowed that. We—I mean *they*—was makin' the fire up and jokin' together. I hollers out, 'Come on down an' git us, Summers!' An' bless Pat, he come right down an' got us!"

We left our own recent federal court jury service with great respect for the justice and humanity of our courts and judges, as well as for the bravery of our law-enforcement agents. The present-day "revenuer," so we understand, goes about his business unarmed, because the unwritten code still frowns on shooting down a man unprepared to defend himself likewise. Too, a murder penalty makes a moonshining sentence a breeze. An able young United States attorney, after convicting a wholesale conspiracy ring of 'shiners, gave a third reason (indirectly) for "better health" among revenue men, though this in no sense reflects on their courage. He said, approximately, to the jury and courtroom:

"I want to remind you all that these men, though they've been convicted as lawbreakers, are in no sense the gangsters and hoodlums of vicious underworld organization. The defendants in this case are plain, decent country boys who just can't seem to realize they shouldn't make a fast buck on untaxed whisky. There is no other count against them. They've owned up to this one. When they learn their lesson—and I believe they will—we won't see them here again."

Every now and then a convicted man was given a choice as to when to serve his sentence. "You say your harvest isn't in yet?"

"No sir, Judge. If I could get my corn in an' a couple hogs kilt—"

"All right, then. Let's say right after Thanksgiving."

"Yes sir. I'd like to spend Thanksgiving with my folks at home. Thank you, Judge. I'll be back here very next day."

The jury felt its responsibility keenly in these cases, but once in a while a touch of humor penetrated its solemn discussion. We remember one staunch fellow who balked flatly at the idea of calling a man guilty of possessing illegal whisky, when the first "drawings" from his still, a sample of which was exhibit A in the trial, was described to us as containing about 9 per cent alcohol. That stuff, the juror declared, was no more whisky than a pigtail was a country ham. We filed back to ask the judge, who solemnly looked up the word for us in the dictionary—a legal one, we are sure, since ours varies—and pronounced it to be technically "whisky."

Famous as Kentucky is for the genuine bonded article, there are a great many of her people who are strict teetotalers, and of her one hundred and twenty counties a little over three-fourths are dry. Imbibers can be found in these areas, but there are also people in wet areas who feel that even Christmas-flavored eggnog or a fruit cake wrapped in a napkin soaked in liquor are questionable indulgences.

CHAPTER 12
Horses, Horses, Horses

---

*O*F GREAT INTEREST to the general run of visitors to Kentucky is the state's fabled horse country. Most of this is situated in the Bluegrass, although there are fine stock farms in other sections as well. If there is anything more appealing to see than a gently rolling pasture in which a dozen or more yearling thoroughbreds are grazing along a wandering creek, we will try to keep open minds. Sometimes these faunlike creatures will group together and break into a sprint, as if they heard some starting signal, and run and run and *run* around the pasture. And if your temptation to open the gate or climb the fence to see them at close hand is too strong, they will come trotting to welcome you, as friendly and interested as puppies.

Some of the big stock farms and breeding establishments are still Kentucky-owned, but others have been bought and developed by Eastern and Western millionaires, and here are such equine princes as Citation, War Admiral, Tom Fool, and others holding court in white-fenced paddock or palatial stable.

The elegance of these domains has been carried to a fine point indeed, the paint spick-and-span, the roomy stalls immaculate, the metal trim and mahogany woodwork polished and gleaming.

If you take a tour of any of these establishments you will,

likely enough, fall into conversation with some knowledgeable
"hard boots" who will acquaint you with various facts and
figures which may be of interest. Did you know that three-
fourths of all the money won on race tracks throughout the
country goes to Kentucky-bred horses? . . . that a yearling son
of Nashrullah out of Lurline B. fetched the record price of
$86,000 at the eleventh horse auction conducted by the Breed-
ers' Sales Company at Lexington? . . . that the stud fee of Nashua
would probably be $10,000 or more for a live foal? . . .

If your interest extends further you may view some of the
farms specializing in horses other than thoroughbreds; there
are ones featuring show horses, three- and five-gaited saddlers,
fine harness horses, trotters and pacers, the roadsters of yesterday.

Several excellent quarter-bred and standard-bred strains of
blood were once developed in Kentucky, when the interest in
them was not merely a thrilling and expensive hobby, but as
practical as operating an automobile agency now.

You can still find "horsy" families in the state, whose "young
fry" are at home in the saddle by kindergarten age and delight
in the blue ribbons they collect from the exhibitions of the
riding clubs which may be found in many towns. But, taken by
and large, it would be difficult nowadays to find that legendary
young Kentuckian who would languish without a horse, a gun,
and a violin.

In some sections the "gentry" still ride to hounds—a few of
them sporting pink coats—and in Lexington the hounds receive
an annual blessing from the Bishop when the hunting season
opens.

Horse shows arouse great enthusiasm, and almost every
county fair spotlights these events. About fifty shows are put
on during the summer, from Paducah to Bowling Green to

Owensboro, from the gala Junior League affair at Lexington, to Harrodsburg, Shelbyville, and Danville.

The tiptop production is, of course, in Louisville at the time of the State Fair, when the world's five-gaited championship is presented on the closing night, with each season's audience hoping for a new Wing Commander, Sweetheart on Parade, or Mass of Gold.

1956 saw the christening of the new Fairgrounds, a plant which cost some sixteen million dollars and covers an area of three hundred and fifty-seven acres. Louisville is proud of this addition to her attractions as its enormous ring offers an ideal setting for full-scale sports events of various types.

Harness racing is currently popular in Kentucky, as in many other states, and devotees who have a feeling for tradition will seek out the grave of Nancy Hanks, the most famous trotting mare of all time, which may be found at Poplar Hill, not far from Lexington.

To some the present-day trots have lost their old-time fascination, possibly because in earlier days nearly every gentleman-farmer in rural Kentucky owned a good trotter or pacer, which he himself drove in the trials, while today the professional driver has taken over and the sport grown to be as commercial as many another.

They're Off!

The thoroughbred racing, spring and fall, at the Keeneland track in Lexington is of great pride and interest to Kentuckians, and the sport of kings as displayed at Churchill Downs in Louisville has attained world-wide recognition with the influx of uncounted thousands of visitors on that first Saturday in May when the Derby is run.

Traditionally, this is the "run for the roses," although Kentucky's home-grown roses don't co-operate. Peonies and early irises are sometimes blooming, and dogwood and redbud often dance along the roadsides, answering spring's sweet call, although occasionally tight buds merely promise that they *will* bloom, or scattered petals on the ground attest that they *have* bloomed.

Louisville hostesses have problems. They haven't heard from all their expected guests. And they *have* heard from unexpected ones—those pleasant people they met in Boston or Benares several years ago—the ones who said, "We've always wanted to go to Kentucky. Someday we'll drop in and pay you a surprise visit." "Pray do!" was the cordial response then. But not now. Not with six seats to a box, and boxes harder to come by than dragons' teeth.

Visitors arrive by steamboat, jalopy, and custom-built convertible, by plane and by daycoach, by Pullman and private railroad car.

Many come on the Louisville and Nashville, which has, in a way, been "Kentucky's own" since the 1850's, when the state was enjoying a breather between the Mexican War and the Union-Confederacy struggle. At that time the newfangled Iron Horse first puffed fire and brimstone through her quiet land, and became a link between the North and South. From the days of the wood-burning engines to the diesel electric giants of today, from the era of the "highball" signal and plushy seats, to the present, when many familiar "locals" have become ghosts, the Old Reliable has brought welcome guests to Kentucky.

Our native sons and daughters love nothing better than an excuse for putting the big pot in the little one, and the influx of country cousins and visiting firemen over the Derby weekend affords an excellent reason for both formal and informal entertaining.

Many businesses arrange lavish parties for their customers. These are usually given at hotels and clubs and have elaborate menus and extravagantly beautiful decorations. But it is the friendly home parties which are much more characteristic of the Gateway City. These feature juleps made in silver cups, preferably sterling, preferably ancestral, and the conversation is spirited and "racey." There is talk of the great horses of the past as well as those of the present.

Lexington, the Granddad of Thoroughbreds who sired 236 winners, is mentioned with admiration as being the most famous stallion that ever lived. Man o' War is given praise. Whirlaway's track record (Derby of 1941) and the names of Citation and Swaps are mentioned for the Hall of Fame, before the guesses begin on this year's favorite, and a half-dozen long shots, which might—just might—outdistance him.

Somebody's sure to tell of that horseshoe of immense American Beauty roses which were carefully de-thorned at dawn, so that the winner of today's classic would feel no prick when they are placed about his arching neck.

And then there's the shout of, "Almost time for the first race! Let's get goin', folks!" and the scramble for transportation.

Although there are many Louisvillians who do not go to the Derby, some being morally opposed to racing, some being hard at work, and others preferring neighborhood television parties, it still seems as if the world-and-his-little-brother are all wending their way in an hilarious tangle to Churchill Downs.

The landmark of the twin towers looms in the distance. The prospect is delightful, the weather divine. Here's the entrance, the Salvation Army lasses with their cheerful tambourines, the touts in their checked waistcoats, the jug band of little Negro boys, grinning from ear to ear, the sellers of balloons and toy horses, and, *look!*, there's Joe Smith whom you haven't seen since college days. Good ole Joe!

Over the archway are the names, written up in bright gold, of every Derby winner down the line. The first one is Aristides ... who's today's champion going to be?

Costumes at the track vary wildly, the more picturesque featuring turkey-red shirts, or pink-and-green plaid, ten-gallon hats, and sideburns for certain gents of the rock-and-roll school. Jockey caps in luminous colors are favorites, and picture hats, trimmed with replicas of the race track, green trees, running horses, starting gates, and all, for the gals.

Orchids by the gross, gardenias by the crate. Oh, my yes! You'd feel naked as a baby jaybird without a corsage.

Things to take? Well, Kentucky weather sometimes being on the temperamental side, you might carry along a raincoat, a hot-water bag, and a palm-leaf fan. You'll need a Racing Form, if you're in the know, and, if you're not, you may do just as well with a black-headed pin to prick the program when it comes to picking a winner.

At hearts-beat-high-time, all eyes are on the gallant thoroughbreds, and a good many on their probable odds. The boxes, the grandstands, the infields are all jam-packed. Everybody's out for fun. And everybody *has* fun!

Suspense builds up all during the early races. And then the bugle sounds with special portent for the Big Race. The band strikes up "The Old Kentucky Home" and a breeze carries the sweet sad melody away, and then brings it back again. The horses parade to the post. Scores of grooms and stable boys line the rail, and perch on the barn roofs across the track, watching their own special candidates caper and sidle along. The jockeys salute the officials, smartly, correctly....

The gate opens, the bell rings, and the thoroughbreds break, stretch out, running, running, running.... Somebody shouts,

"Here he comes, he's making his bid! Look at that! Just watch him run! Did you ever see the like? I knew he'd win—hoped he'd win—and he almost did!"

Well, maybe next year *your* horse *will* win.

Horse-and-Buggy Days

The town of Lexington is the hub of the big irregular wheel of the Bluegrass, and is its big city, center of its business and social life. A rambling beautiful old town, she has a special air of graciousness, of gaiety and assurance. A historic town, she numbers among her landmarks Mary Todd Lincoln's birthplace, Henry Clay's Ashland, Transylvania, first university west of the Alleghenies, and the John Hunt Morgan House.

She's a college town, home of the University of Kentucky. And she's a country town, delightfully so. Horses and tobacco are of great concern to her, and so is her social life, and she possesses a particular style and finish, and her ways are worldly and leisurely.

Called the Athens of the West from her youngest days, she has many narrow old streets with charming old, old houses and public buildings, as well as fine new ones. Her native son, Gideon Shryock, distinguished architect of the 1830's, designed some of her older structures, among them the lovely Morrison Chapel at Transylvania, as well as the courthouses at Louisville and Frankfort, and the old Statehouse with its famous double circular stairways—all these of Greek Revival influence.

Lexington used to be known familiarly as Chittlin' Town, too. Chitterlings, in case you don't know them, are the cut-up small intestines of pork, fried a crisp—and they say delicious—brown. Burgoo is also a favorite dish traditionally, probably originating in Virginia. It is a very tasty soup or stew, made of game meat originally, cooked for hours with every vegetable in the garden—of tame meat more lately, still cooked for hours with all vegetables available—and highly spiced always. It has long been a popular feature of the horse sales, the Bluegrass Fair, and any barbecue in that neck of the woods.

Bluegrass food is hard to equal. A few tried and true specialties are the dainty lace-edged corn cakes, "real" corn pudding and its variant, a delicious soufflé in which the corn is grated; beaten biscuits, not overdone and hard-tack-hard, or crumbly as crackers, but a little *al dente* as they should be, served usually with thin slices of old ham; ambrosia; mayonnaise, very firm, and made with olive oil and lots of lemon; a waxy fruit cake whose base is a pint of chewy cherry preserves; hot soda biscuits; black bottom pie; an incomparable spiced tea; a whipped cream candy coated in thick bitter chocolate; and Bibb lettuce (developed in Frankfort) with a lemon-garlic dressing. . . .

All the people of the Bluegrass towns and the counties in and around the region are noted for lavish entertaining and much foregathering. Everybody knows everybody else, who they were for generations, and a good deal about their ways and means. There are easily more Kentucky cousins per square mile than there could possibly be cows in Texas.

The rolling land of the Bluegrass, the spacious open woodlands, the rock fences or whitewashed paddock ones, or even the rugged old stake-and-rider or rail kind, the dense mock-orange hedges, famous Shady Lane and others like it where trees meet overhead to make an endless leafy tunnel, the sweet old houses behind their avenues, the pastured horses and contented fat cattle—oh, it's all idyllic, reminiscent in its perfectly groomed green neatness of an English countryside, and fostering a horse-and-buggy atmosphere that has much appeal.

Though Kentucky's early roads were dreadful, the nineteenth century developed a system of toll pikes that were somewhat better. With unlimited limestone handy, these were practical, and many of the early winding little pikes are still extant, though the main thoroughfares have happily become concrete or black-top highways long since.

In the hey-day of the pikes, white swirling limestone dust billowed after the fast buggies and carriages rolling back and forth to town. The chief use of oil, then, crude oil, that is, was to spray the pikes to keep down the ankle-deep dust. No sanding was done in horse-and-buggy days, the black crude oil being sprayed on and left to wear in.

Oh, the delicate problem of a Victorian lady's stepping up on that tiny little iron step of a buggy, keeping her long full skirts off that high sharp-rimmed wheel with its thick icing of ruinous black oil, without displaying more than an inch or so of well-turned "limb"! Oh, the mountainous washbaskets filled with froths of petticoats and embroidered frilly drawers sadly smirched with sticky black oil. Lard rubbed into the stains was the one remedy to soften up the dreadful stuff, and pounds of it were patiently applied. When the starchy ruffles came back from Mattie's they were usually perfect again—but many a washboard or beating stick was worn out on them, and many a fluting iron patiently turned mile on mile and hour on hour.

Today's tourist, driving through Kentucky, will see many reminders of the Victorian era in fretwork added to the porches of simple pleasant houses and, if he happens to visit with an old-timer "sitting out" here and there, will hear some stories of ingenuous pleasures of an elaborate yet uncomplicated age when Kentucky Country had some enviable folkways indeed.

One custom, in general practice in the eighties and nineties of the last century, was for every family within reasonable distance of the farms of their relatives to arrange visiting schedules for all the children cousins. What an idea! And how the young loved it. This custom is said to have started around Mayfield in southwest Kentucky, but it must have spread like wildfire, for it was a state-wide movement.

The highly practical idea—a change of scene every week or so for the young, and a quiet summer for the elders, except for their one super-active fortnight—is probably the forerunner of today's popular summer camps.

Yesterday's children considered the eight-mile trip to Aunt Margaret's quite a jaunt. Each place they visited offered new adventure, but the ways of life were much the same. A couple of big bedrooms, or perhaps the whole attic, of each comfortable country house would be arranged dormitory fashion. The carpets and rugs had been removed and cool summer matting put down. Trundle beds, pallets, and cots were ready for the bigger children; the little ones, three or four to a bed, were given the big testers and four-posters.

Aunt Margaret's candle flickered in the breeze and cast pleasantly scary shadows on the walls as she came up to say good night. (The young had gone to bed by the last rays of daylight.) She heard everybody's prayers, and then entertained with a bedtime story or two, sometimes about the mule that could open all the gates on the farm, but more likely about some family saga—the time Cousin Jeff, one of Morgan's men, riding a coal-black steed, his saddle blanket of scarlet sheepskin, rode all night to bring his sweetheart a birthday rose. . . .

A great favorite was the story of Little Arthur who naughtily disobeyed his pappa and went into a forbidden field to slide down the straw stack there. In sliding, he woke a bad-tempered bull (Pappa's wise reason for suggesting that he stay out of the field), asleep in the shade of overhanging straw. The naughty lad was not gored, though his listeners always expected and rather hoped he would be, but punishment was automatic. He scrambled to safety on top of the straw stack, *and there he stayed.* (One felt she would surely add, "To this very day.")

No one heard Arthur's cries, and hungry, burned by the sun, and chilled by the night rain, he stayed, the bull below keeping a baleful eye on him, Search parties beat the bushes everywhere, but *nobody* (till next day) dreamed of looking for Arthur in a place he had promised his dear pappa not to go. . . .

As a matter of fact, there were few taboos—except the well and the barn roof—imposed on the young visitors. Before automobiles, they could range at will. There were usually a few ponies or a gentle saddle mare or two to ride, and there were acres of field and stream to explore, seesaws to improvise on any fence, hours of croquet, and the recurring fascination of helping with the milking, riding the work horses to water in the pond, making chewing gum of fresh-thrashed wheat, catching chickens for the cook, and making snakes of horsehairs.

The older young people, and the young older people, had their own version of these house-party visits. A tallyho with seats enough for several young couples, and one married pair to chaperone them, was the popular vehicle, a day-and-night stay the usual visit at the several country places on the schedule.

One story that came to us concerns a smart coach with crimson wheels that matched the livery of its groom and bugler and was truly drawn by four white horses. Hampers of delicious food were produced for al-fresco luncheons in sylvan glades on the way, and banjos, guitars, and mandolins were used to accompany the singing as the leisurely miles melted away.

At every tollgate along the pike, the bugler executed a flourish to bring the keeper on the run to unbar the way. Children and chickens scattered and everybody stared as the elegant equipage dashed past, bonnet ribbons whipping in the breeze, handkerchiefs waving, laughing voices floating back. Every vehicle on the pike gave room to the gay processional, and there was many an envious backward glance, too. . . .

At each house to be visited, lawn-tennis parties or receptions had been arranged, with a hop or cotillion or "German" for entertainment during the evening hours, and other diversions next day.

Group horseback rides at dawn or by moonlight were popular with everybody, or bicycle tours under blooming locusts, croquet tournaments, charades, woodland picnics, an afternoon at "the trots," a fish fry at the river, hayrides, buggy races.

"What they used to say about those days was probably true," we were told wistfully by a very old lady. " 'Heaven must be a Kentucky of a place!' "

Kentuckians have always been greatly concerned about Heaven, we may add. And when the requisites for getting there became a matter of real disagreement in a church, the usual solution was for one group to break away and start another branch, same denomination. As far as we can find out, Kentucky's record along this line is unrivaled.

Feelings could be sulfurous on the subject, too, as in Monticello, when the Christian Church some years back had two branches, one banning music from its service, the other going so far as to organize a band. A member of the sterner branch, hearing the trumpets sounding forth from the Sunday school basement one evening, said to a friend on the street corner, "There they go, tootin' their way to hell!"

Another Monticello story of the period concerns a Presbyterian congregation who "unchurched" one of their members when he insisted, after a visit to New Orleans, that he had seen ice made out of water in the middle of the summer. This was so flagrant a lie, the elders agreed, that his name must be stricken from the rolls of the elect. Everybody knew pond ice kept pretty well through the summer, in an icehouse full of straw, but that was quite far enough for human beings to go, it being only in the province of God to *make* ice.

But when the preacher himself made a trip a year or so later and reported that he too had witnessed the phenomenon, the ousted brother was taken back into the fold.

A good many Kentucky Country people have never quite gotten over the wonder of ice made at home in the summertime, for electric refrigerators, quite as often as washing machines, are the chief adornments of the front porches of many a roomy cabin home. So is gone much of the drudgery of horse-and-buggy days.

But their leisurely pace is forcibly restored, at least momentarily, in the hamlet of Kuttawa, and by a modern convenience too. In the outskirts of either end of town, far from any intersection, is a traffic light that stays red nine-tenths of the time, successfully slowing down thousands of horsepower to a gentle jog trot.

CHAPTER 13

A Mighty Scope of Land

"Bold Headlands and Pilot Knobs"

*P*ERHAPS THEY ARE high hills rather than mountains to the true geographer but they stand out in sharp contrast to the gently rolling countryside they guard. Rugged areas crop up all over Kentucky, but her eastern highlands, taken as a whole, cover nearly 13,000 square miles—almost a third of her land—a section about the size of Massachusetts, Connecticut, and Rhode Island together. Thirty-five eastern counties are mountainous, the two big ranges, the Cumberland and the Pine, rising about four thousand feet in height. Here the picturesque scenery abounds in bold headlands and pilot knobs, with gorges and rapids and waterfalls.

This country has typical mountain flora. The ridges are covered with pine and chestnut and an undergrowth of huckleberry. Trailing arbutus drapes the cliffs, and laurels and hemlocks flourish as do rattlesnakes and an infrequent bear.

If you are "high-minded" you can take a tour in a loop beginning and ending at Louisville, going to Mount Sterling and finding the first rise of the mountains fifteen miles from there. Salyersville is the start of the steep hills and then comes Prestonsburg and Dewey Lake, the Big Sandy Valley and Pikeville. On to Breaks of the Sandy with its spectacular mountain gorge, back to Pikeville and Allen, then west to Dwarf. After that comes Slade and Natural Bridge State Park, and nearby Sky Bridge in Cumberland National Forest. From there the road leads to Winchester and so back to Louisville.

A longer swing of an added hundred-odd miles includes Cumberland Gap and the Falls. On it you will see Big Black Mountain, the highest point in Kentucky, and pass through Pineville, Middlesboro, and Corbin, returning to Lexington and back to Louisville with memories of unforgettable scenery and friendly folk along the way.

The inhabitants of the highlands have been called our contemporaneous ancestors for, in spite of considerable recent progress, a few of the older people still cling to the era of the bull-tongue plow. A few women in the remoter sections still card wool and spin and weave and, in doing the family wash, "battle" their clothes with a stick in a nearby spring.

Having never been slaveholders, mountain men were generally strongly Union in the War Between the States. Their loyalty was a byword in more recent wars, as they topped the rest of the state and the country in voluntary enlistment. Always they have made fine fighters since the days when they came to grips with General Zollicoffer at Wildcat Mountain and struck a blow against the Confederacy.

In the five-volume *History of Kentucky* edited by Judge Charles Kerr, the authors William E. Connelley and E. M. Coulter say: "Whether at New Orleans under Jackson, at Lake Erie under Perry, at King's Mountain under Shelby, on the battlefields of Mexico, in the Indian warfare of the Revolutionary times, or under George Rogers Clark in opening up the Northwest Territory, or the Great World Wars, these mountain men have always shown that bravery under fire, that loyalty to their commanders, and that true marksmanship, that have ever characterized the bravest of the people of any time or age."

The people of the Cumberlands are largely of English and Scotch-Irish blood. Woodrow Wilson stated that in these mountains could be found the original stuff of which America was made. Cecil J. Sharp, the British folk-song authority, writes that, although many of these people are uneducated, they "possess that elemental wisdom, abundant knowledge and intuitive understanding which only those who live in constant touch with nature, and face to face with reality, seem to be able to acquire."

Their speech is flavored with many of the words which Shakespeare used, and with those found in the King James translation of the Bible. Some of these expressions may also be heard in "hillbilly" spots of western Kentucky, where the earliest settlers had the same Anglo-Saxon heritage and were isolated on the far rugged side of the Green, the Cumberland, and the Tennessee, or near the Obey River.

Here certain of the older folk "allow" that such-and-such is so. They say something is "right smart" this or that. They greet you with an invitation to come in and "set a spell" or "take the night." They are feeling "peart" or "right tol'able, or "fair to middlin'," unless they have the "mis'ables." They are "afeared" or "beholden," as the case may be. They "fetch-an-carry," and they "holp" one another. Salad is "sallet," just as it was in olden times, and a bag is a "poke." "Clumb" is the past tense of climb, and "et" is used for ate, as it often is in England and Canada.

There is a certain charm about these archaic expressions, a nostalgic and atavistic race memory, perhaps, which unites us with our forebears and makes us feel a closer kinship to them, as well as to these, our neighbors who are proud to be addressed, when aged, with the ancient courtesy title of "Aunt" and "Uncle"—a title of accorded dignity and respect due their gray heads and mature philosophy.

Old Ballads

The greatest contribution of the mountaineers to the state's store of culture is to be found in the beautiful weaving and in the ballads, handed down from one generation to another, many of them reminiscent of Mother England's "North Countrye," a land famed for its minstrels. In many of these ballads names have been localized but the original theme is always preserved.

Jesse Stuart has made the mountain life of today breathe for all of us in his books. John Jacob Niles has sung the mountain story in this land and across the sea and has made some rare finds among the half-forgotten songs of an early day. Among the best collections are the "Traditionals" published by Josephine McGill some years ago; and also noteworthy is "The Singing Lady," compiled by Jean Thomas, who wrote *Blue Ridge Country* and has done so much to preserve and popularize the original ballads and recognize the modern adaptations; those of such as Jillson Setters and others, which "larn" us that the creative spirit is still "on the wing." Indeed, though most contemporary "pomes" are about "Pore Young Tom" or Dick or Harry, who well deserved his penitentiary term, there is a suggestion of Robin Hood, Kentucky being particularly susceptible to hero worship of "boys in bad with the Law."

Once we had a Jesse James, and there were those Victorian misses who admired his winning ways. . . .

Cayce Jones was a Kentuckian, born in Cayce, near Fulton, and we still chant:

"Come, all you rounders, if you want to hear
A story about a brave engineer,
Cayce Jones was the feller's name,
An' on a big eight-wheeler he won his fame...."

Elmer Griffith Sulzer, whose *Twenty-five Kentucky Folk
Ballads* was published by the University of Kentucky, says in
his introduction: "Kentucky, without doubt, possesses the
greatest wealth of folk ballad material of any state of the
Union."

Among the songs he chooses for inclusion are "I Gave My
Love a Cherry," "King William," "I'll Give You a Paper of
Pins," "Froggie Went A-courting," "Barbara Allen," and the
well-known "Tree" with its branch and twig and nest and egg
and bird and feather.

Some of the old ballads are decidedly earthy. In mentioning
"Ida Red and Ida Blue, I Love Ida Same as You," a footnote is
given: "Only the chorus of this rather popular little ditty can be
included in this collection. Those knowing the words of the
verses will need no further explanation"—which, we would
assume, is a classic of understatement!

The twenty-five verses of "Young Charlotte" tell of the sad
fate of the maiden who lived "in a wild and lonely spot" with
not a dwelling within five miles "except her father's cot" which,
being "a social abode," "attracted the swains on many a wintry
night," since Daughter was very fair.

It transpires that young Charlie's sleigh dashes up to the door
on New Year's Eve and he proposes that they go to a merry ball
in a village some fifteen miles away, for "though the air is
freezing cold as death, our hearts are young and light."

Fond Mamma suggests that her ewe lamb bundle herself in a
blanket.

" 'Oh, mother dear,' " the Daughter said,
And she laughed like a gypsy queen,
" 'With blankets all muffled up to ride,
I never shall be seen.

" 'My silken coat is quite enough,
You know it's lined throughout,
And here I have my satin shawl
To wrap my throat about.' "

After five miles at a jaunty pace her companion remarks that
the ice and snow are freezing on poor Charlotte's brow and her
denial of this fact is somewhat fainthearted. When at last they
reach the festal scene he tries to hand her out of the sleigh but
she sits there like a monument.

In verse seventeen:

"He called her once, he called her twice,
She answered not a word,
He asked her for her hand again,
But still she never stirred."

Verse twenty presents the climax:

"Then quickly to the lighted hall,
Her lifeless form he bore,
'My own, my only true, true love,
Your voice I'll hear no more.' "

The twenty-third verse presents the traditional ending:

"They mourned for the loss of their daughter dear,
Young Charlie mourned o'er his doom,
And at last his poor heart did break,
And they slumbered in one tomb."

Do those of you who are past your middle years remember the
penny dolls of your early childhood, those stiff little china
poppets holding their arms tightly glued to their sides? And
did you know that their "official" name was Frozen Charlottes?

Aunt Sukey's Cabin

The charm of these folk stories in rhyme and the simple grace of their singers touch the heart with tenderness and transport the mind to the Elizabethan age which originated many of them, for here, in the isolation of the Appalachians, there still remain some fastnesses which, even today, have been over-looked by modern progress.

If it would "pleasure" you, you may join us on a visit to one of these spots. Here, up the creek a country mile, is the log cabin where Aunt Sukey and her bearded, bright-eyed old husband, Uncle Hanse, have lived since they were a fifteen- and sixteen-year-old bride and groom. The logs are chinked with clay and the huge fireplace where the cooking is done takes up one wall. Above it hangs the powder horn and the long rifle which Uncle Hanse's great-grandpappy used when he was a sprig. Half the room is given over to Aunt Sukey's four-harness hand-hewn loom. She bids you set in the rocker and begins to talk.

No, she don't use the loom no more, but she did when she was spry. In her mammy's day all the flax and wool was come by at home. Her mammy was a great hand at making coverlids. "She grew the madder that made the red dye, prettiest dye that ever was. But she had boughten colors, too, indigo and cochineal and all. See in this chest are the kivers she made. You aim for me to call you off some the names of the patterns?"

You nod and finger the sturdy softness of the old pieces. Words like warp and weft stir in your subconscious mind as you see and feel the complex cross of thread over thread.

"This here's Dimonts," Aunt Sukey explains in her reedy voice. "Then there's Pharaoh's Wheel, and Gentleman's Fancy,

Blazing Star, Whig Rose, an' Chariot Tracks. All them ole-timey patterns is pretty."

Aunt Sukey smiles and rocks, rocks and smiles. A rare moment of leisure and friendly talk this is, and she is enjoying it to the utmost.

We examine the "kivers" which she has heaped in her lap, and accord warm admiration, marveling at the richness of their glowing colors, the infinite variety of imaginative pictures they present.

We have brought Eliza Calvert Hall's *Book of Handwoven Coverlets* as a present for the old woman, and, at her urging, a bit of this is read aloud to her—a quotation from an editorial writer in the *London Nation:* "In certain primitive and necessary things there lies an irresistible appeal. We perceive it in a windmill, a water-mill, a threshing floor, a wine press, a cottage loom, a spindle, a baking-oven, and even in a pitcher, a hearthstone, or a wheel. There we see the eternal necessities of mankind in their ancient, most natural form, and, whether by long association with the satisfaction of some need, or simply by their fitness for utility, they have acquired a peculiar quality of beauty."

"Hit's true," Aunt Sukey comments, "although hit's right fanciful."

She closes her dim old eyes to study the thought for a moment, and then goes on, "You want me to spell you out some more of the patterns? I could keep hit up day-long. There's Cat Claws, an' Governor's Garden, an' Olive Leaf, an' then there's Rose in the Wilderness, Winding Vine, Forest Wonder and Orange Tree, Parson's Beauty and King's Delight, Lonely Heart and Indian Camp, Birds of the Air and Floating Wave.... Did you ever hear so many?" she asks proudly.

Lonely Heart and Indian Camp, Birds of the Air and Floating Wave—the very names are a song in themselves, and behind each name there must be a story—dozens of stories. Women bending low over their looms in candlelit cabins, women sleeping at night beside their beloved husbands, women lying awake in the lonely darkness. . . .

Aunt Sukey runs a roughened finger along the lines of print in her gift book and studies the pictures intently, her face brightening as she recognizes and names many of the designs.

She tells us that only the old-timers like herself and a few of the neighbor women can weave so pretty. Some of them were taught by trade weavers who went from place to place with a pack on their backs. Yes, ma'am, she's heard about the new craft centers which have been set up in some of the counties, to revive the old art. But she doubts if these new boughten dyes they use nowadays will make the colors lasting and rich as the ones her grannie taught her to make when she was a young thing. . . . Peach leaves and smart weed were best for yellow. Hemlock, butternut, and maple could be used for gray, and when you wanted red you could melt block tin in "strong water." Wood berry made a right fair blue, though indigo was better, if you could come by a pinch of it.

When it came to "bilin' up" the mix, and dipping your stuff, you had to keep faithful watch, and never take your eye off the bubbles in the black iron pot. Your hanks must simmer so long, no longer, till they were colored strong and clear, but not too brash.

Aunt Sukey keeps up the "floating wave" of her rocking, the rhythmic cadence of her talk: "Strip the bark of blackjack. When hit's on the rise in the kittle, add a nubbin of alum before you douse your yarn. You'll have green then. Iffen hit's black you're wantin', take some warnuts, or some shumake berries. Larkspur's mighty useful, an' bloodroot. Sweet laurel is, too, an' sass'fraz. The good Lord put all them yarbs aroun' fer us to seek an' treasure. . . ."

"Drafts?" Why, her grannie had a "chist" brimmed with them patterns, she tells us, and hobbles across the room to search them out for us. They are strips of tow linen, patched and backed with yellowed paper, worn with handling throughout the years, until the marks on them, which look not unlike a music score, are almost illegible. Here are the directions for threading and setting up the looms, for the art of doing this task is a difficult and intricate one. . . .

"Look a-here!" Aunt Sukey says. "See what else I found in that ole chist. Hit's the Dream Book I uster read when I could see good. The things hit tells must be true because they're writ down in print. Some of them is the same as those my great-gran'pappy tole me by word of mouth. An' they're all true, every last one!

"To dream of apples means that your sweetheart is faithful an' will never court another lass. . . . Here, Woman, you line hit out to me. I've dis-remembered all the book larnin' I uster own."

And then, before the reading can begin, Aunt Sukey decides to call in Uncle Hanse, so that he can share this pleasure with her, as he has shared all others, during the more than fifty years of their marriage. She rings the cow bell from the rickety little porch and this summons him from the nearby turnip patch where he has been working.

A plate of corn pone and a jug of buttermilk make their appearance, and when the "vittles" have gone the rounds, the reading begins: " 'A candle snuffed out foretells sickness and, maybe, death, but a bright, unblinking flame means rejoicing to come—most likely, a speedy wedding. A golden chain predicts many children.' "

"See here, now do!" Aunt Sukey undoes the top button of her decent blue calico, and shows us *her* chain. "Hanse guv it to me when Brother Nathan joined us together." She smiles at the old man, who nods proudly, and tells us that they had twelve children, adding that there were only a couple left now out of the whole batch. "Two-three, that's all, an' them in a far-off place," he says sadly, "far's I know . . . t'others died a-bornin'."

Two or three left out of twelve. That was the usual story in these hills in the old days. . . . We tell Aunt Sukey goodbye, holding her frail hand for a long moment, as Uncle Hanse goes back to his work.

One Woman's Vision

Now the remote-hill picture of maternal welfare is very different, thanks chiefly to one woman's vision, and the organization which has developed from that vision. This woman is Mary Breckinridge, descendant of a Kentucky family which has played a prominent part on the stage of public affairs for many generations.

After the loss of her husband and two dearly loved children, she took back her maiden name and studied midwifery. Thus equipped, and with private means and boundless energy, she started the work which was later to receive world-wide recognition as the Frontier Nursing Service.

In the fall of 1926 a beginning was made with two nurses and a rented house. Soon afterward a log house and barn were built at Wendover in Leslie County. Throughout the winter the midwives rode from one lonely cabin to another, fording icy streams, climbing steep peaks, teaching a better way of life as they gave their services. Later a hospital was built and the settlement boasted two of the five baths to be found in the county.

In the intervening years the work has grown and prospered.

Now approximately six hundred square miles is covered by the services of these dedicated women and nearly ten thousand people have benefited from their bedside nursing, obstetrical care, and public health work.

These nurses have had greater odds to fight than the difficulties of mountain travel, for the isolation of the Kentucky mountain country has proved a hotbed for the breeding and preservation of many odd superstitions which the mothers cling to with tenacity. Many insist that a pan of burning chicken feathers must smolder beside an ax under the bed during childbirth, also that the husband's hat—usually none-too-clean an object—must be worn at this time. Snuff blown in the mother's face through a goose quill is considered efficacious, as is the chewing of dogwood berries.

If the baby develops thrush—pronounced thrash, in mountain parlance—a local granny-woman suggests that a horse should breathe into his mouth. If this doesn't effect a cure she insists that a neighboring thrush-doctor be called in. This individual must be a seventh son or a seventh daughter, or else a person who never saw his or her father. The treatment is the same as that administered by the horse. A good long puff is supposed to do the trick. Seven will do it more quickly, no doubt!

If the baby has a birthmark, the accepted belief is that this can be removed by touching the spot with a dead man's hand. Chills can be cured by letting the youngster suck a daddy-long-legs rolled in dough, and if there's trouble when teething days come along you can (if you want to) try rubbing rabbits' brains on the gums.

Many of these remedies, as well as the customs and folkways surrounding them, are a direct inheritance from the days of Good Queen Bess. So, too, are the mores and philosophy of the people who hold them.

An Eye for an Eye

In Mary Breckinridge's *Wide Neighborhoods* she tells us that because the pioneer code is still usual in the mountains of Kentucky, stealing is here regarded as a greater crime than shooting, since the thief loses social caste while the killer does not.

This brings us to the much-publicized institution of feuding which, in the past, was prevalent in many mountain counties but has been "out of fashion" since World War I when horizons were broadened and a younger generation was freed from the shackles of inherited bitterness.

To most of us all feuds are typified by the famous Hatfield-McCoy Affair which Virgil Carrington Jones characterizes as "not just a tragic quarrel between two backwoods families, but a strife that eventually developed into a dispute involving two states."

The scene of the warring clans was the borderline between Kentucky and West Virginia, near where Tug Fork flows into the Big Sandy. The Hatfields lived over the stream in West Virginia and the McCoys on the Kentucky side.

The trouble began shortly after the Civil War under the aegis of Devil Anse Hatfield and Rand'l McCoy, who had fought on opposite sides, and was carried on by their numerous progeny—each of them having thirteen children, as well as nephews and cousins galore. No account of the number of killings was kept, estimates ranging from twenty to more than a hundred. Any spark was enough to kindle a flame. Once there was some question about who owned a hog, again it was the Romeo and Juliet affair between Rose-Ann McCoy and Johnse Hatfield.

In 1880 it was a batch of gingerbread that started the fracas. It was election time, always a good excuse for a free-for-all. The

McCoy lasses, on their side of the Tug, offered a free treat to those voting the ticket which their own menfolks favored. The Hatfield lads, on the lookout for trouble, crossed the river, and, although it was clear they had no chance to vote in the neighboring state, made free to sample that gingerbread. They were challenged and charged with banding together for the purpose of annoying and disturbing the peace.

There were fireworks then, and the little brown jugs passed from hand to hand, followed by much flourishing of shooting irons. Those Hatfield boys dared the sheriff to try to take them in. But that gentleman valued his life more than his career.

And then, again, election time came round. Phamer McCoy began the battle this time, and it ended in the death of Ellison Hatfield. The murdered man's clan killed three of the McCoy boys to prove that they meant business. Twenty men were indicted but, after an interval, the clerk of the court noted in his entry book the names of these twenty, all followed by the significant phrase, "Not found in this county, February 19, 1883."

During the following years, rows of notches appeared on guns and many bearded giants were missing-and-presumed-dead. Rand'l's house was fired and his daughter Allifair lost her life. The governors of the two states took a hand in the investigation of the "alleged outrages" and stiff official messages were exchanged before the Hatfield Lords of Creation were rounded up by the law and shipped to Louisville via the Chesapeake and Ohio railroad. The *Courier-Journal* had a "scoop" by sending a reporter aboard, but he was "taken for a ride" in more ways than one, as the group presented a picture of injured innocence, denying that there had ever been any but the friendliest relationship between themselves and their good neighbors, the McCoys.

The prisoners were exemplary inmates of the jail, enjoying divine services and serenading the other prisoners at 4 A.M., their accustomed rising hour, much to the local felons' discomfort. They were eventually sent back to Pikeville for trial and some received penitentiary terms, only to be pardoned before their expiration.

A recent writer in the *Courier-Journal* says: "If all the words written about this feud over the long years were laid end to end, they undoubtedly would reach from here to the Tug and back again in an unbroken chain of distorted facts and half-truths. . . . Few, if any, have tried to connect the conduct of the McCoys and the Hatfields with their environments and to show them as men who reacted to certain situations exactly as did their Scotch and Irish ancestors during the fierce Highland wars in the old country."

And what of today in the land of feuds? All is peace? Certainly—except for a caper every now and then, for in recent news from Jackson, situated in "Bloody Breathitt" County, we note that targets have been painted on tombstones in the cemetery and the sound of midnight "pings" proved annoying to neighboring householders. The entrance to the graveyard is to be padlocked and chained, the key being available only to funeral directors and mourning families.

Mountain men are great lads for tricks and pranks, and at times can outsmart your city slicker.

Take the hillbilly boy and the bee trees, for instance. Not too long ago anyone finding a bee tree in the big woods could lay claim to its harvest, and mark that claim by initialing the bark.

This stripling, who was a stranger in the neighborhood, boasted of his extraordinary good luck in finding some fifty trees. These he was willing to sell at a bargain price of three dollars each. If his customers wished to examine the trees, they were at liberty to do so. It was likely each one held more than a hundred pounds of sweet'ning.

"Take this one, now," he told the gathering crowd. "Just see them swarms of bees a-buzzin' out of the hole!"

Blue-jeans pockets were emptied fast and there was a land-rush business before the lad left town and it was discovered that the sample tree had been merely plugged with honey and a comb, and the busy little insects had been carrying off the treasure instead of stashing it away.

Hill folks may appear lackadaisical at times, but when they have a job to do they can put their backs to it. A recent newspaper article noted that twenty women from Pike County aimed to shame their local politicians who had failed to keep election promises, and they did just that. There were forty-eight families along the narrow road that led to the schoolhouse. The ruts and washouts made it impassable to any wheeled vehicle, yet nothing was done about it.

Last election day they'd had a promise that it would be repaired and black-topped. That promise, it seemed, was like pie crust, made to be broken, and the children had to "walk the trail" to catch the bus to take them to school at Belfry, until the mothers got busy and put in a couple of days of hard labor with pick and shovel. . . . P.S. One month later an anonymous manufacturing firm has lent a newfangled machine which will lay down a six-inch base and give these Amazons a road that can be traveled twelve months a year—"United We Stand."

And, surprisingly enough, Kentucky, in spite of her contradictions, past and present, *is* united, although one commentator states that, like the proverbial Gaul, it is likely to be regarded by outsiders as being divided into three parts, industrial Louisville, the "Kodachrome" horse-racing Bluegrass, and the "gun-totin' " mountains.

This is oversimplification, certainly, and presents a false

picture, for Louisville is still a "big-little" town, the fabulous Bluegrass doesn't even look blue to some color-blind eyes, and a director of mountain missions of the Southern Baptist Church states that the 7,000,000 people who live in "Appalachia" are endowed with "such sterling qualities that once they are led to give their hearts to Christ, there can be no more loyal and faithful Christians to be found anywhere in America."

Our mountaineers are a kind and generous people and their "neighborliness" is proverbial. Take Uncle Lester, a lonely old codger, who inquired daily for mail at the crossroads post office, even though he had never received a letter within the memory of the settlement's oldest inhabitant.

Somebody thought he should—and that somebody did something about it, for on the old man's eightieth birthday the smiling clerk handed him more than a hundred cards and letters. Uncle Lester returned all but one of these to the clerk and now they'll be given out to him on a weekly basis, and he won't hear the familiar, "No letters for you today, Uncle Lester," for a long, long time to come!

CHAPTER 14

Big Lakes and High Hills

ALL ACROSS KENTUCKY'S southern territory, from the mountains in the east to the very Purchase in the west, is the new man-made lake country. Because of her happy combination of rivers and high hills, Kentucky has the perfect setting for these enormous impounded lakes, made by damming the rivers at strategic points, the water backing up into reservoirs against the walls of the hills.

Electric power and light, and flood control, too, were the first concern in this change of the face of so much of the land, but the end results—another case of the tail wagging the dog—have been startlingly rewarding. Not only have the lakes meant recreation for millions, but they have brought tourist money in huge quantity to sections where this commodity had been pretty scarce.

Old King Coal

Now the mountains of Kentucky, both eastern and western, have great natural resources, much of this untapped. Besides the oil, ores, timber, natural gas, and saltpeter produced for years, there are unknown quantities still to be developed. But the first big industry of the hills was that old monarch, Coal, with his merry smile, and an extremely black scowl too.

Here in the most beautiful surroundings imaginable one comes on the drabbest dump-heap villages and the neatest busy towns. Many a shirt has been lost and many a life, too, on the "black diamonds," but there never was a person from mountain areas (if there are any we haven't met 'em) who hasn't an abiding respect for the industry, and who hasn't gambled with it, or wanted to, in some way. In spite of market slumps, a fluctuating demand, strike problems, and mine disasters, coal has a very real pull for the children of its discoverers—land leaser, mine owner, or pit miner.

Unhappily for the early settlers, not one of them realized that fabulous unsuspected riches lay under the trail to the Great Meadow. But for their descendants who chose to stay in the hills, the finding of coal, much later, often meant a fortune overnight in the sudden increase of land values. Not always, by any means, but it did happen many a time. It also meant an accessible supply of fuel for nearly everybody, for a lot of coal was at surface level, with plenty more farther down.

Coal brought in railroads and developed a prosperous shipping center in Corbin. It had a lot to do with getting roads into mountain regions, too. We well remember Harlan in the period before World War I, with coal money pouring in and more fine automobiles proportionately than any other Kentucky town. The trouble was that the only paved road was a few-mile stretch through town and out a "little piece." In bad weather the fine Stutz Bearcats and other contemporary models zoomed back and forth on this one solid road, day and night, pacing tigers, effectively barred from roaming.

Tax money and pressure on the legislature changed all this, and roads were under way right away. Coal affected everybody in the hills in some way, but the big dammed lakes have been even more "influential" for they bring together so many, many people in pleasant personal relationships, even while they nourish the horde of new big and little business ventures— resort cottages, fishing docks, restaurants, filling stations, bait and tackle stores, and so on.

Same Way Up Here

Time was when the truly rural mountaineer and the lowland "furriner," rural or not, viewed each other as different breeds of cat. Now it is rare indeed that any visitor with passable manners encounters the suspicious, strong-silent character of cartoon life. Local fishing guides on any of the big lakes now are proud of the visitors' delight in the great beauty here, and are extremely talkative and friendly, matching story with story, easily having the last word.

Of course the wide travels of some of the young guides who have seen war service in World War II and in Korea have made them more cosmopolitan than a good many of their customers. And the thorough opening up of the once fairly isolated, rugged country has given the tourist a better realization and appreciation of the people who live in it.

Rural electrification as well as the business and pleasure of the huge recreation centers is appreciated by the people most affected. But some of the older ones still grieve over their own Lost Atlantis, as a veteran fishing guide once told us, in his own moving way:

"This here's deep water under us, mebbe couple hundred feet 'long here. See that road yonder, where the water breaks it off? That was a raght nahce road. Hit wound on down in the valley to a—well, hit wasn't a *town*, just a little place.... But it had a real perty church, an' some raght nahce houses, an' buryin' ground an' all.

"I mind old man Greenup, he wouldn't b'lieve his house was goin' to be drownded out. They kep' tellin' him, an' reasonin' 'bout it. He wouldn't move. Not him! They had to come an' take him away. Hit don't seem right, somehow, movin' off an' old man by force, when he never wanted 'em to. . . . He drownded hisself raght off that point. I reckon he was plain out determined to go home."

"That was too bad," we tell him, sincerely sorry. "But a great many other people must have wanted the lake, didn't they?"

"Mebbe so." His eyes meet ours in defensive brooding, and we feel very much the outsiders for a little while.

We think then of Harley, guide for a hunting party made up of several couples, a few years ago. He disapproved of women in the group for one thing, and of "sports" in general, and showed it by refusing to make any positive statement. Was it going to rain? Mebbe. Was this a good duck cove? Could be. Had squirrel hunting gone well this year? Yep an' nope.

A jack pot was made up, and won finally by the one man to get a free-wheeling flat statement from Harley. On one drizzly morning the women urged the men not to go out. One husband suggested sweetly but firmly that the ladies seek a warmer climate—*they* were going hunting.

"Harley," he said, becoming conscious of a flicker of surprise in the guide's eyes, "in the low country where we live, when we tell our women what to do, they *do* it!"

And Harley snapped back, "Same way up here!"

Often a touching folk tale of close personal nature comes from our mountains. Years ago when the Society for Crippled Children was being established, H. V. McChesney of Frankfort, a moving spirit in this fine work, persuaded many a truly remote high-hill family to allow some child who needed surgery to come down to the hospital and be given a chance to walk. One youngster gave him a somewhat startling version of the New Testament story, very much in his own words:

"Wasn't it awful what they done to God's boy?" (In the mountains it's still so and so's "boy," rarely "son.")

In the startled silence, the child went on. "They kilt him. Some mean ole men shot him with a forty-four. . . . You think it hurt him none? Well, it never! He's a mighty fine man, they say, and alive and well today!"

A story in a different vein was told us by a Lexington friend, Mary E. Sweeney, educator and writer, who once visited the Frontier Nursing outposts and was to spend a night in a mountain cabin.

"Please," one of the nurses reminded her, "don't forget to *show* how you practice the 'last rites' of brushing your teeth, combing your hair, bathing. We preach it all the time, but object lessons do help, and this is a very simple household you're visiting."

Her bedfellow that night was a bright little girl of seven, who hopped in bed without ceremony when the rest of the family retired to the loft. By the dying firelight Miss Sweeney proceeded to brush and *brush* her teeth, comb and brush her hair thoroughly and long, scrub her face and hands, undressing and slipping into her gown leisurely, hanging her clothes neatly over a chair.

The little girl, all eyes, was hunched up on the bunk bed, in silent attention. Then she *had* to make a comment. "Stranger," she said, "you be a heap o' trouble to yourself, ain't you?"

Berea to Renfro Valley

With so many inaccessible districts, the three R's have too often been just a little too hard to come by for some of the mountain people. A scarcity of books and a long hard trip, miles of it, every day and often on foot, have been a barrier for all but the most determined. An enlargement of the school program and our recent and thoroughly extensive Bookmobile Project are turning the tide.

Back in the early 1900's, Mrs. Cora Wilson Stewart, herself a mountain woman, and a brilliant one, made the first successful move to reach the children, and their parents as well, by starting neighborhood schools to appeal to both. "Moonlight Colleges" she called them, and the special readers she provided —*The Country Life Readers*—were an inspiration. For a man to set aside his pipe to read, "I see kitty," was embarrassing. In the new reader, under a picture of a road, would appear the lines, "This is a road. Mountain people need good roads...."

One of the great bulwarks of higher education for mountain people is, of course, Berea College. There are many others now, but Berea was the forerunner. Established in 1855, the College Department added in 1869, Berea admitted colored students along with the white, the earliest of such ventures. The school has high standards and draws its present 1,500 students chiefly from the 230 mountain counties of eight Southern states. It charges no tuition and only nominal board and fees, and *all* students take part in an admirable and fair work plan. The student industries are an interesting part of this splendid old school—among them Mountain Weavers, Woodcraft, Fireside Weaving, Broomcraft, and so on.

The outdoor theater there is magnificent. Set at the Indian Fort, with real hills and real trees, and even real vines wreathing the few excellent facsimiles of rock headland used in the staging of Paul Green's "Wilderness Road" pageant, it is one of the most atmospheric amphitheaters in the country.

On down the highway a very few miles away is an interesting institution of a different nature, but with plenty of traditional flavor. Here dulcimer playing, the making of ballads on the spot and the singing of old ones, the delights of the old-fashioned "set dance" or square dance have been preserved for the enjoyment of everyone. This notable stronghold of mountain lore is John Lair's Pioneer Museum and his big barn at Renfro Valley, where Kentucky's "contemporary ancestors," as up to date as the latest airplane model, still gather to enjoy the old-fashioned recreations of *their* ancestors, a rich heritage of all Kentuckians, along with tourists from every state and many foreign countries. This is commercial, too, having popular radio and television programs, but it is based on the real thing.

Near it and its attractive chink-log cabins are true "first-time" log houses, built before the nineteenth century, staunch, splendid with a particular dignity. In Mr. Lair's ballad book, *Songs Lincoln Loved,* we find a bridge from the very old to the perennial favorites of today.

"Revive Us Again"

The state of Kentucky, in her younger days, was full of grandiose plans for universities and colleges, some of which materialized. But it must be admitted that it wasn't only the hill country with its scattered population, but the growing cities as well, that were a trifle slow about getting a sound elementary program of education going.

Schools were established, of course, but the legislatures were parsimonious with the tax monies. Private schools were set up by "p'fessors," some of them very good ones. And after the Southern fashion, a family prosperous enough employed a tutor for the children. Thomas Nelson Page as a very young man once tutored in the Brown family of Jefferson County.

There were "blab-schools" wherever there was enough support to keep one going. These were usually started by the churches, who were strong "voices in the wilderness" demanding a good free school system.

Actually it wasn't until 1869 that enough taxes for a widespread school program were voted. Even so teachers were scarce and their salaries inadequate. This story is a familiar one today, but the standing of the public schools is generally creditable. A recent illiteracy study put fewer than 5 per cent of the people in this unhappy category, and special effort is being made to brighten all the corners where they are, through an "Each one teach one" campaign.

Kentucky, both town and country, is a land of churches, the country ones especially having been original centers of community, civic, social, as well as spiritual life. A "powerful preacher" has always had great appeal here, from camp-meeting days on.

The rampaging emotional orgies of the early nineteenth-century camp meetings got decidedly out of hand. Wagonloads of followers came along for the free fish fries and basket suppers, and to "shout up" the congregations. Teams of preachers, a half dozen or so, harangued the crowds, one taking up when the last fell exhausted to the sawdust. Giant bonfires gave an eerie effect to the stampings and rollings and shoutings.

There are still "old-fashioned revivals" but the frantic sawdust trails have faded away like four-mile races and asafedita bags.

Statistics show a general increase in church membership over all the nation, but in the Kentucky hill country the percentage has always been high. At the hundreds of little wooden meeting houses anywhere and everywhere, many a hitch rail has a few horses and mules lined up, along with the automobiles. Often one minister serves several churches in turn and on "preacher's day" everyone around turns out, for though a mountaineer may need his boy for farm work too badly to send him to school, it's a rare one indeed who doesn't see that his boy has a chance to "wrestle with the Devil" and hear the Holy Word.

Let's Go Fishin'

As a practical-minded local schoolmarm once told her class, "It isn't necessary to give me a Christmas present, but many children *do!*" So we and many thousands of others feel about fishing in any of the lovely, lovely lakes round and about.

There's Herrington in the middle, the oldest one, built in 1925 by backing up the waters of the Dix (or Dick's, for it once belonged to an Indian chief of that name). Then there's giant Kentucky Lake made by the Tennessee River, in the Pennyroyal, this one two hundred miles long and twenty wide in spots. There's Lake Cumberland in southeastern Kentucky, and arms of Tennessee's Dale Hollow in the mid-south, and many lesser ones.

Each lake has its special charm. As the waters backed up to create them, filling valleys and pushing into hollows and clefts in the rocky hills, some of those mysteriously blue ridges one sees while driving through mountainous country are the new shores of the big lakes. The mountains have been brought to the tourist, for his little boat, thanks to rising waters, has been floated up to these very ridges and fastnesses, and wonderful they are at close hand.

Here, for example, on a long sandstone and shale point, terraced weirdly with great rock slab formations and gravel "spits," a boat can be tied up. One steps out easily onto the stair-step bank—a perfect spot to cook on the rocks. Behind the rock point rises the wooded hillside, probably to a sharp ridge a hundred feet higher, once many hundreds of feet above the valley below.

Here are tree and bush, wild flowers beyond imagination, lady's-slippers, a strange delicate wild orchid, wild honeysuckle, masses of wild plum and crab, sweet William, the pale smoky rockets of "sarvis" trees, dogwood of course and redbud and calico bush (laurel) and all the old familiars, poppies, wild hyacinth, bittersweet, spicewood, holly, "cowcumber," columbine, foxglove, and the most lush pillows of moss of a hundred fascinating varieties.

Fishing in the big lakes can be exceptionally good, if the time is right. As any fisherman knows, the fish were usually striking best last week, or ought to be about ready to jump next month. But if there is anything more rewarding than a nice fighting small-mouth caught on a surface or deep-running lure, just off a gravel bank in clear green water with a background of sheerest beauty, we are open to suggestions....

Besides the enormous impounded lakes, there is one natural one, the Kentucky part of Tennessee's Reelfoot Lake down in the Purchase. Here some interesting wild life has made a successful last stand along the ravines and shallow marshes of this weirdly lovely swamp lake.

Here wild grains and Indian rice lure every waterfowl that crosses the country. In the dank green and sunless fingerlike lagoons and inlets (very much like the Louisiana bayous) are found all sorts of lizards, turtles, mink, beaver, otter, muskrats. Game fish—black bass, both large- and small-mouth, walleyes, and bream—like the protection of the thousands of dead trees, drowned there a century and a half ago, their twisted skeletons still standing there.

Kentucky has her full share of drawing cards in her varied state parks (Natural Bridge, Cumberland Falls) but it's the big lakes with their hundreds and hundreds of miles of secluded shoreline that offer the most to the most people, and not merely to the fishermen, either.

There are plenty of other attractions—boat rides, camp trips, swimming, hiking, horseback riding—with accommodations from air-conditioned lodges and charming rustic cottages, with last-word kitchenettes, to six-by-eight shacks with bunk beds only. But just one vacation trip to any of these lake-cloud-and-mountain retreats becomes a magnet.

It's a powerful pull, from a first glimpse through a gap in the hills as one approaches to the last look on leaving. We remember one night of yellow moon and mist curling like cream in iced coffee. We watched the color change, the murky water become black satin as the mist rose and the moon silvered over. A night bird made a shadow-quiet flight into a thin pine treetop.

We sat in the car at the top of the long hill drive, looking down at the dock. It was cheerful with lamp (electric) light and boats coming in, croppie fishermen going out with bright lanterns for some night work, voices warm and idle-sounding. Way up the cove we could hear and presently see a hurrying outboard, a noisy, busy sewing machine stitching black and white ruffles in the water.

And while we dearly love *our* neighborhood, *our* county, *our* happy city home, it was just awfully hard to go back to it.

CHAPTER 15

Kentucky's Underworld

The Word Is Speleologist

OR, IF YOU PREFER IT, you may choose spelunker, if you are an explorer of caves.

We can be sure that legendary Houchins, who in 1809 stumbled into Mammoth Cave in pursuit of a bear, didn't call himself anything half that fancy. Likely, he just called himself unlucky—and probably "scairt."

Let's go through that historic day with this Long Hunter, who we shall assume actually was the first white man to glimpse the stunning surprise of the cave, although from time to time his claim to fame has been questioned since it is said that records at Bowling Green show the cave property was marked as a corner of a section of land in 1797. However, there is no mention of any knowledge of the exploration of this cave, so we may choose tradition for our story and Houchins for our hero.

We picture him waking in his lean-to shelter near the spot, stirring the embers of his watch fire to a brighter glow, spitting and broiling the couple of varmints which are all that remain of yesterday's meager hunt. These he sprinkles with a few frugal grains of precious salt, as he dribbles spring water over his last handful of parched corn and downs the feast with hearty gusto.

His deerskin leggings and fringed hunting shirt are damp from his sleep on the dewy ground and he's glad enough to grab his Betsy rifle and tramp into a clearing in the Big Woods where the warmth of sunshine cheers his heart, game or no game.

Day-long, let's have this fellow hope for luck and then, his hunger sharp as the keen edge of the scalping knife that swings at his side, we are with him as he hears a snuffle and a grunt in that big hollow tree yonder. His eyes glisten and he draws back into the brush, tiptoe wary as the bear sniffs and snorts, lumbering out of his refuge.

Already Houchins feels his moment of triumph. Already his palate tickles with the anticipation of those roasted paws, hot, juicy, succulent!

He tracks Bruin for a time, then stumbles after him down into one of those bushy sinkholes with which this land is pitted. It's dark here. You go down, down, down! Yonder yawns a cave.

He can't see the bear but can hear him somewhere on ahead, tumbling rocks, pushing them aside with his huge clever paws. Houchins won't give up. Not now. Not ever. He kneels, takes flint and tinder box, and manages to spark the handful of dry moss he carries in his pouch. In the brief moment of flame he glances upward and his unbelieving eyes are stupefied by this vast cavern in which he is lost.

We may suppose that he forgot the bear, forgot everything but his longing for his familiar world of trees and sky. Maybe he said his prayers. Maybe he cursed. No one knows what kind of man this Houchins was. We like to think he got his bear, feasted royally that night, and dreamed ever afterward of the wonderland he had glimpsed.

Fawn-Hoof

In her book about Mammoth Cave Helen F. Randolph says that Mammoth Cave was hoary with age before the Greeks worshiped Zeus and the lesser gods in their cavern temples, that the Water Clock here marked time before the Oracle of Delphi gave messages to the votaries. The Giant's Coffin stood here before Lot went up out of Zoar, and the Grapes of Proserpine "forever ripe and forever unplucked, were hanging in the underworld of Mammoth Cave before the myth of Demeter's daughter and the pomegranate inspired Greek poets or Orpheus sought Eurydice."

Speaking in less poetic terms, we may say that Mammoth Cave dates from the carboniferous era of the Paleozoic age of more than a million years ago. It is situated in Edmondson County, approximately a hundred miles from Louisville, in what has been called the most remarkable cave region of America, an area made up of eight thousand square miles, six thousand of which are in Kentucky, the other two thousand in Tennessee and southern Indiana.

There are hundreds of caves in this district, some small and some large, many well known and others unexplored as yet. Each year brings forth a fresh crop of spelunkers whose spirit of adventure inspires humdrum stay-at-homes.

From time to time new discoveries have been made in Mammoth Cave itself, new depths plumbed, new avenues opened up, unexpected relics discovered.

Perhaps the most romantic of these discoveries was the mummy which was found between 1813 and 1816. The figure was that of a young woman, taller than average, dating from some prehistoric age. Her features were regular, her hair dark red, shorn to a short cap over most of her skull. Her deerskin robes were dressed in a fashion different from any recorded method, and she presented a mystery which has never been solved. She was christened "Fawn-Hoof" because, in certain dimly remembered legends, the red hoofs of the fawn are said to be symbolic of innocence.

She was found—and she was lost.

She was found by two men who were mining saltpeter in a recess of the cave which was later to be called Gothic Avenue because of its groined ceiling. This passage is forty feet wide, fifteen feet high, and two miles long.

Fawn-Hoof's sepulcher outstrips in grandeur that of any of Egypt's queens. The theory has been advanced that she was an Aztec or an Incan maiden because some of her accessories were not unlike those found beside Peruvian mummies. Her seven feather headdresses and deerskin mantles, the hoofs of fawns, the claw of an eagle, two rattlesnake skins, a dark cap and reticule, seven quilled headdresses, needles of horn and of bone, bunches of deer sinews, dozens and dozens of seed necklaces, and, to give her enchantment in the after life, two little whistles or flutes—all these lay beside her.

She was dead too soon, surely, for she was young and, we surmise, beautiful. Her hands were folded across her bosom in that eternal sign of rest and peace. She must have been loved for she was buried with care. But the hatred she found must have been greater than love for there was a gash between two of her ribs. Punishment? Revenge?

Her wrists were bound with a cord and she was wrapped in a double layer of deerskins which were shaved parchment-clean and printed with a pattern of whitened leaves and vines. These were encased in a square of woven or knit fabric which was like the matting made from the bark of a tree grown in the South Sea Islands.

It is not believed probable that any chemical process in the cave could have reddened her hair, and the theory has been advanced that her auburn tresses may have been shorn at the time of her death and possibly worshiped in some religious rite.

Some ethnological experts hold that the Indians were not the first inhabitants of Kentucky, but that a "cultured and gentle" race may have preceded them, and that this race was vanquished by hordes from the north. It is said that this tradition was fostered by the Indians whose legends told of a final stand here where the cavern offered refuge.

Shortly after her discovery Fawn-Hoof vanished as completely as the history of her countrymen. Within five or six years after she was found, she became the Lady Who Wasn't There Anymore. Some said she had been presented to the American Antiquarian Society. Some that she had been given to Peale's Museum. Others claimed she had been given to a Mr. Ward of Massachusetts. Others were sure she had found a final home in the Washington Museum. Or was it the Smithsonian? Or the British Museum?

Fawn-Hoof, who were you? Fawn-Hoof, where are you— where is the dust that made your body, the laughter that lifted your warm lips, the tears that brimmed your innocent eyes— where is your immortality?

All these questions are just as unanswerable by us, today, as they were unanswerable by those two forgotten men who discovered the mummy a hundred-and-fifty-odd years ago.

Wonder of the World

These miners were not bent on exploration but were "spelaeans," as they lived underground for months at a time, working the nitrous earth for saltpeter to be used in the manufacture of gunpowder for the War of 1812. The cave and its sixteen hundred acres of land had been sold the year before this for the sum of forty dollars. It changed hands several times but by 1837 was well known as one of the Wonders of the World. Its first two guides, Stephen Bishop and Matt Bransford, not only made wonderful discoveries of their own, but also established a hierachy which lasted for a number of years, many of their descendants being numbered among the intrepid guides and explorers from that day to this.

Bishop was a slave who belonged to the owner of the cave. He was supposed by some to be part Indian, having the look of a Spaniard with long, slightly curling hair and a black mustache. He had an immense chest and strong shoulders, and his slouch hat, green jacket, and striped trousers made him an ornamental figure. He taught himself the fundamentals of geology and many notable scientists listened to his cave theories with respect and admiration, making him a partner in their explorations into unknown netherlands, since his skill and bravery were equal to any emergency.

When guests from all over the United States and many foreign countries were not engaged in traversing the underworld they made themselves at home in the historic old log hotel which, tradition says, ranked in comfort with the Louisville Hotel and the Galt House. Its timbers were hand-hewn from the nearby forest trees, and it stood, staunch and sturdy, for a hundred years until it was destroyed by fire in 1916. Its spacious façade was six hundred feet wide and its rambling verandas presented a fine view of cultivated flower gardens and natural woodland. Early guidebooks drew particular attention to the ballroom where "hoop-skirted beauties forsook the bloomers of the cave to dance the old-time waltz" to the strains of music provided by a first-class orchestra.

These books also gave advice on cave etiquette. One, written in the late fifties, says: "The Bloomer or Turkish trouser is the proper costume for a lady and, when trimmed in lively colors, the effect is beautiful. Every lady carries a lamp, and in no case, except that of illness, should she take a gentleman's arm. It is fatiguing to both parties and exceedingly awkward in appearance."

It was also suggested that the fair sex should attach small silver bells at neck and waist and wrist, in case their delicate footsteps should lag behind the sturdier strides of their male companions.

In these early days the magic of Jenny Lind's voice floated out over Echo River, Booth recited Hamlet's soliloquy in the Amphitheater, and Ole Bull touched the strings of his enchanted violin in the great concert hall which was christened in his honor. Emperors and grand dukes supped in the Banquet Hall and wandered, as awestruck as ordinary mortals, through the temples, some of which are two acres in extent.

In Italy a young Louisville physician was asked so many questions about Mammoth Cave that he was embarrassed to acknowledge he had never visited the marvel. On his return home he was so impressed by its splendor that he bought it and spent large sums of money developing its scenic beauty.

Visitors are always impressed by the fact that the temperature does not vary but remains around fifty-four degrees, this is because the air currents are expired in the summer, when the outer atmosphere is hot, and inspired in the winter when it is cold. There is little life in the cave and no light. Here, says Bayard Taylor, hours have no meaning and time ceases to exist.

More than a hundred years ago a group of medical men developed the theory that the unvarying temperature and the absence of dampness and dust would prove to be of value in the treatment of tuberculosis, and gathered together a company of patients to test the curative properties of the cave.

A row of canvas-roofed cabins was erected beyond the Grand

Bend, and here the hopeful ones made themselves at home, attempting to while away the idle days with music and gossip, with letter writing and light exercise. Some of them were companioned by members of their families and faithful servants, all of whom must have found the lonely life dull and dreary. One misery and danger which had not been anticipated was that in the breathless atmosphere the smoke from the numerous supposedly airtight stoves hung in stagnant clouds, aggravating the patients' coughs and irritating their afflicted lungs.

There were ten patients living in Mammoth Cave during the autumn of 1842, one of these a four-year-old child. One young man wrote a letter which is quoted in the *1946 Filson Club History Quarterly*. He says with pathetic gallantry: "I am not sure that anyone has grown better but all concur in the opinion that they would be worse out, and hence contentment generally pervades our little community."

For a time some of the patients did seem to improve, but after several months their faces became ashen from lack of sunlight, and all of them died within three days to three weeks after leaving the cave as their weakened bodies were unable to adapt themselves to a return to the upper world.

Dear Courtland—And Lost John

It was in this same pre-Civil War era that one young Louisville miss wrote in her velvet-bound diary: "Dear Courtland! He is the most Beautiful and Spirited Young Gentleman I have ever Encountered."

She was merely one of this "Romantic's" innumerable admirers, for the young man was truly a darling of the gods, seemingly fated for early death that overtook him in the first engagement of the war.

He was the son of George Dennison Prentice, editor of the *Louisville Journal,* whose name was known wherever newspapers were read and witticisms quoted. He shaped the public opinion and politics of his day and it is said that he, more than any other man, influenced Kentucky's decision to side with the North during the War Between the States—this in spite of the fact that his two sons fought with the Confederate Army.

Courtland was killed after a month's brief gallantry, fighting with Morgan's Cavalry. After his death, at the age of twenty-six, the *Louisville Journal* said of young Prentice: "He loved to seek the wildest and loneliest portions of Kentucky. Repeatedly he went far up among the bald and desolate crags of Dix River, a region haunted by the bear, the wildcat, and the catamount. The piercing scream of the panther was a sound of rapture to his ear. He was ever in search of natural curiosities, and he discovered caves previously unknown, in all probability, to any man of our generation, and in one of them he discovered immense quantities of human bones that seemed to him to have belonged to a different order of human beings from any now upon our continent. He subsequently became as familiar with Mammoth Cave as the best of its guides. An adventure of his in the subterranean realm attracted world-wide attention."

This reference was to Courtland's descent into the Maelstrom, or Bottomless Pit, a feat that has rarely been equaled in the succeeding years, having been undertaken only twice since then before it was forbidden by the authorities. He was the first man—actually a teen-ager rather than a man—to attempt this perilous undertaking which had been considered impossible.

This pit "yawns for twenty feet amid wet and slippery rocks. . . . Deep, dark, and terrible, it lies, a source of mystery, at the end of the longest avenue in Mammoth Cave, nine miles from the entrance, and thus presents, as it were, a fitting climax to the grandeur of the cave. Of the tens of thousands who have gazed into its depths with awe, while Bengal lights thrown into it seem but to intensify its terrors, only a scant handful has even desired to explore its black gulf," says Helen Randolph.

Of these Courtland was the first. He procured the longest, toughest rope available and rigged up a set of pulleys and a basket on September 11, 1852. The rope was tied around a large rock and swung back and forth in the pit to dislodge any loose fragments. Several fell and the thunder of their reverberations echoed upward.

The lad pulled several caps over his head, took his light from the guide, fastened the rope around his body, and swung out into space, directing the men to lower away. Rocks and earth tumbled around him but none of the debris struck him. On the way down he was drenched with spray from a cataract but managed to shield his light.

He landed on the floor of the pit which he judged to be about eighteen feet in diameter. He examined the snowy quartz formations, scratched his name on the wall, and shouted for the guides to raise him part of the way up to where he had noticed a recess he wished to examine.

When Courtland reached this level he swung himself into the recess, but, as he did so, the rope slipped out of his hand and dangled beyond his reach. His friends above were unable to help him in any way.

Edging cautiously to the very lip of the shelving rock, he reached out his lamp hook, and these few added inches made it possible for him to catch the swaying rope. After an investigation of the chasm which had interested him, he shouted to Stephen Bishop to pull him up as he fastened the rope about his body, quickly, carelessly. It pinched him as he swung out over the abyss, trying in vain to shift his body weight.

And then the torture of the pain was forgotten for, as he hung midway in the vacuum of the Maelstrom, swaying with every tug of the rope, he heard a shouted alarm from above that his lifeline had caught fire from the friction of the pull over the timber around which it was wrapped.

For the watchers the agony of suspense was almost unendurable until someone grabbed up a water bottle and managed to douse the smoldering strands, while the others continued the steady pull-pull-pull which brought him, after an eternity, safely to the top.

"Thanks!" said Courtland cheerfully. "It was wonderful. You can't think how grand!" He peeled off his caps and mopped his face, and then he saw that one of his helpers, a middle-aged professor, had fainted and he turned his attention to help revive the man.

This daring exploit of young Prentice's was celebrated in a long, long poem by the Reverend George Lansing Taylor which remained a popular schoolroom recitation for many years. It was intoned with suitable gestures and "elocutionary eloquence":

> *"Into the dark profound,*
> *A deep that plummet ne'er did sound:*
> *Still he descends,*
> *And anxiously bends,*
> *Gazing down into darkness that never ends,*
> *Whose dimness,*
> *And grimness,*
> *And darkness,*
> *And starkness,*
> *And deepness,*
> *And steepness,*
> *And deadness,*
> *And dreadness,*
> *More fitful are made by his lamp's sticky*
> *   redness...."*

And so forth, and so forth, *ad infinitum!*

We turn with pleasure from this strained effusion to choose a few of the lines which George D. Prentice wrote after his son's death:

> *"Dear Courtland, thou, the strong, the brave,*
> *Fillest a warrior's bloody grave....*
> *Bright ones will sigh, the young, the old,*
> *When thy sad destiny is told....*
> *Thy name high hearts will love to keep,*
> *Through all thy lone and solemn sleep."*

We would like to think that the beneficent spirit of gay young Courtland presided over the wedding ceremony of the couple who were married in the Gothic Chapel of Mammoth Cave in the summer of 1870. We are told in the old records that the bridal party walked eighteen miles underground before returning to the hotel for the reception. Did the bride wear those Turkish trousers, we wonder, or did she trail a white-satin train through Fat Man's Misery and the Corkscrew Turn?

The cave has been the scene of tragedy as well as high adventure and romance. There must have been many, unknown to history, but one will serve as a symbol of all, and here is the story of "Lost John."

Some years ago one of the professional guides crawled between two rocks and laid his hand on what he thought was a rounded stone. It turned out to be the skull of an Indian who must have met his fate here some five-hundred-or-more years ago.

The find was reported to the National Park Service and an archaeologist studied the skeleton and deduced the theory that this man, whom he christened Lost John, had been collecting gypsum, possibly to be used in some religious rite. In his hand he had held a reed torch, by its uncertain light moving from one narrow ledge to another, a cautious foot trying out each dangerous step before he shifted the weight of his taut body.

Wearied from his search in the darkness of the labyrinth, this John had laid down two bundles of oak sticks and a handful of reeds, and composed himself to eat his lunch of hickory nuts. Perhaps he daydreamed for a moment before he dropped the empty shells, visualizing his triumphant return with the gypsum which would make him the hero of tonight's feast. The Shaman would honor him. He would have a double portion of meat. His chosen women would come to him. . . .

Torch in hand he crawled down the steep ledge toward a pile of gypsum under a slab of limestone. He knelt on the ledge to chip it with his stone knife, shifting his left foot for a better stance. The movement, the push of that foot, dislodged the keystone under the great slab which pinned him with a giant's hand.

Perhaps his death was mercifully quick, perhaps slow agony as his unanswered screams changed to rhythmic moaning and he died as the light from his torch died in a last flickering gasp. Lost John found no honor that evening, five hundred years ago, but he has achieved immortality, of a sort, as his skeleton lies there, in state, viewed by thousands, year in, year out.

CHAPTER 16

More Caves

Lure of the Unknown

THE UNENDING STREAM of tourists goes on from one season to the next. Not only does Mammoth Cave invite their interest, but many other nearby caves tempt them to prolong their visit and admire the peculiar attraction which each new vista offers. Hidden River Cave beckons the explorer, and Colossal Cavern cannot but impress even the most heedless for its dome is said to be the greatest natural or artificial vault in the world.

Great Onyx Cave boasts of its translucent stalactites and stalagmites, and Mammoth Onyx Cave of its crystal encrustations, travertin, and coral. Nearly a dozen others, each with some particular charm, are found within the region and it is still surmised that there may be new worlds as one discovery leads to another. Only recently Martian-looking skin divers made an unsuccessful attempt to squirm their way through a subterranean channel, searching for an underwater entrance into one of the caves. These divers, clad only in rubber suits, eeled through a knife-like slit which led downward into muddy blackness from an entry on the bank of Green River.

The expedition's aluminum boat pushed through a twenty-foot passage to Pike's Spring. The tenders in the boat reeled out their ropes to the two venturesome boys who, like Courtland Prentice, were teen-agers. They made preliminary explorations and reached a pool with boundless sides before they had to retreat and acknowledge that the water was too cold.

They plan to make another try, hoping, as all explorers do, that next time they will have better luck, remembering certain chance discoveries in the past.

Take Proctor's Cave, for example. It was found in 1863 by one Jonathan Doyle, a slave who left his master, a Baptist minister, to join the army of Buell and Bragg. In a couple of days he tired of the discipline, of the food, and of the smell of gunpowder and turned his dusky face toward "ole Marster" in search of "forgiveness and pork chops." But, as he neared home, his conscience smote him, and he decided to wait in the woods beside the path which led to the schoolhouse where he could intercept one of the children of the family and discover what his reception was likely to be.

Jonathan sat himself down on a rock to rest and regain his courage. He felt a cooling breeze which seemed to come out of a crevice under his hand. He had lived in this cave region all his life and knew that this must denote an underground draft from a passageway. He marked the spot and waited for his "little Missy" with some impatience and an eagerness which was justified when he was received by his master as a prodigal son.

Keeping his secret, he borrowed an ax from the toolshed late that night and returned to the spot which he had marked. It would have been a good plan to have had some powder and a sledge or drill, but, since Jonathan had none of these aids, he used his mother wit and his strong right arm. Knowing that limestone will crumble under a good hot fire, he chopped down a tree, cut it into suitable lengths, and made a good bonfire. After a while some of the embers trickled down and that crack rimmed out into a hole, a hole big enough for a man to ease through.

It was lucky for Jonathan that he'd thought to bring Master's old iron wick lamp, a "borrowed" scoop of grease, and a hank of rags he'd happened on, there in the toolshed. Wriggling down through the hole, he found himself in a passageway. He crawled along it for hours, discovering pits and chasms, domes and labyrinths. How Jonathan ever managed to find his way back to his entrance and emerge from his underground wonderland remains a mystery, but history records that for many years thereafter he guided visitors through the cave and fired their imaginations with thrilling tales of its discovery.

Salts Cave offers a challenge to scientists and has been called "the cradle of man in America." Possibly it is larger than Mammoth Cave but it has not yet been fully surveyed. A mummy was found there about 1875 and since that time it has held special interest to those concerned with paleolithic archaeology. Many of its winding passages show signs of having been used as streets by a race of people somewhat shorter than the Indians of today, and in several of the cave rooms articles such as moccasins, headdresses, woven bags, wooden bowls, and torches have been found.

One of the many scientists who have made studies of this region has said that Kentucky cave country was an ideal site for prehistoric man because of the heavy forest growth, good fishing and game, a supply of flint, essential in the manufacture of weapons and tools, and an equable climate.

The Floyd Collins Saga

Just as Jonathan found his cave by chance, so, too, did the Collins family, who were log-cabin farmers in the same area.

One day in 1917 Lee Collins and several of his nine children were examining the traps they had set out in the hope of supplementing their income. One of the traps, set in a sinkhole, had disappeared. Evidently it had been pulled down into a vent by the struggles of some small animal. This suggested to them that there might be a cave under this spot.

Standing there in the brush, Lee poked the hole with a stick, stared doubtfully at his son, Floyd.

Floyd nodded. "I aim to have a try, Pa. Might be something big in it for us. Anyways, I like crawlin'."

"We'll need help, son. We ain't got money to chance."

"We'll have to do some tradin'," Floyd said. "The ole sow. Maybe the calf, too. We oughta go ahead!"

Lee shrugged and, with the younger children tagging them, they went on home and made plans.

Before the long weeks of grueling labor were done, the Collinses and the neighbors who had been hired to help with the digging and blasting knew they had a big job on their hands, but at last their entrance was made and they slipped down through the shaft, merely hopeful at first, then unbelieving as the glory of what was later to be called Crystal Cave burst upon them.

The cavern where they stood was a hundred feet long and thirty feet wide. There Lee found his trap holding the torn foot of the ground hog which was the true discoverer of this amazing underworld.

Floyd Collins became a guide and devoted his life to further exploration of the cave, finding new passages and risking his life often in that strange fever of expectancy which possesses every Columbus.

By 1922 he was exhibiting more than ten miles on the upper levels as well as the lower passages. It was his dream to find a better entrance to the cave, possibly a connection with nearby

Sand Cave. He had been working on this project for some three years when, on January 30, 1925, an Edmondson County correspondent reported to the Louisville papers that Collins was trapped in the cave. His family, it was said, was not particularly worried about him, for he had been trapped several times before, once for as long as forty-eight hours.

Floyd would work himself free, they insisted. He was a good cave man, patient and careful. He wouldn't panic or lose heart. A real plucky fellow. He'd make out all right. Just wait and see!

And it looked as if his folks knew what they were talking about for next morning in Louisville the *Herald* ran a headline: "Collins Free—Vows Never Again."

Sometime later in the day the news was flashed that this was a mistake. His brother, Homer, and his father, Lee—Leonidas, his real name was—had crawled down the dark, slimy passageway and talked to Floyd but hadn't been able to free him from under the rock that pinned him down. Maybe it wasn't going to be so easy, even with other folks' help and interest.

And by this time there was plenty of interest for, in this accident, there was an appeal of theatrical drama which excited a news-hungry public. Many people got a vicarious thrill out of the thought of an underworld of eerie mystery. What were the thoughts of the trapped man? How strong was his faith? How great his chance of rescue?

These questions all presented themselves to a young reporter on the *Louisville Courier-Journal* and he was determined to find answers to them. His name was Williams Burke Miller, but he was called "Skeets" because he wasn't much bigger than a mosquito—five feet tall, with a weight of 110 pounds. Skeets arrived on the scene shortly, and Homer told him if he wanted a story he could go down in that hole and get himself one.

As Skeets told the story afterward, he butted around inside

the entrance for quite some time before he got his bearings in the low tunnel, and was able to inch forward through the muck. He called to Floyd but there wasn't any answer. After a while he reached a sharp dip and slid down it against a wet mass which groaned and moved. The shock of the surprise hit him and, as he said later, "I laid my head down on top of that mass and, in my fright, I imagined that I, too, was trapped."

In a moment Skeets pulled himself together and pushed back the burlap sacks which Homer had brought Floyd to cover his face to protect it, in some measure, from the constantly dripping water.

There wasn't anything the reporter could do to help. He left the victim and worked himself on up out of Sand Cave with the resolve that he wasn't going back down there. If he could have been of some use. But he wasn't—and he'd had all he could take.

He telephoned his story back to his city editor, climbed into a hotel bed, and went to sleep. The minute he waked a plan came to him—a harness could be rigged up and the man could be pulled loose. Skeets went back into the cave to suggest that to Floyd.

"I'd rather lay here dead than have my foot pulled off," Collins told him and Skeets had to accept that decision.

The next day thousands of "thrill-seekers" crowded the entrance, for the story rated page one in all the papers in the country.

Skeets went back to Floyd three times in the next five hours. He carried with him a string of electric lights. He held Floyd's head on his knee and fed him soup through a rubber tube. He "managed" a crowbar through the narrow tunnel and tried to raise the rock enough to slip a jack under it.

The jack slithered in the slimy sand. He tried again and again. Again.

"Go rest," Floyd whispered. "Come back!"

Outside Skeets found a horde of newspapermen who charged that this whole show was a hoax, a publicity stunt to widen the circulation of the *Courier-Journal*. One of the Chicago reporters said Collins was crawling out through another entrance every night, returning each day to meet Miller. Skeets didn't say much. He got what rest he could.

On Wednesday, February 4, Collins was fed for the last time. Another rock had slipped and a barrier was formed in front of him. A coal miner from Central City crawled in with Skeets, who was making his seventh trip in three days. They asked Floyd how he was.

"Come on down—I'm free," the man told them weakly.

"If you're free reach the bottle of milk I've placed in the crevice over your head," Miller said.

After a moment of silence Collins told them he wasn't free—and always that last conversation will remain a mystery. Did Floyd really think he was free? Had he been dreaming that he was? Was it a grim joke at the gates of death?

For twelve days after hope had been given up work was continued on an outside shaft while a military probe was under way to determine if the entire affair was a hoax. Miller's hours-long testimony made it clear that there was no trickery involved and that Collins had been trapped in the cave as represented.

The coroner identified the body when it was reached and it was decided to seal it in the cave. A reporter made pictures for nationwide use and turned one spool of film over to a youthful aviator by the name of Charles Lindbergh who was waiting to fly it back to a Chicago paper. He was given a blank and so, for once in his life, that earnest young man failed in his mission.

Several months later the Collins family moved Floyd's body to a grave near the entrance of Crystal Cave and later it was moved back into the cave and displayed in a glass casket.

Up-to-date Spelunkers

The 51,000-acre Mammoth Cave National Park area still attracts many thousands of tourists yearly.

In 1954 a group of twenty-five men and five women arrived under the auspices of the National Speleological Association to attempt a project unlike any ever undertaken before. Their plan was to spend a week in Crystal Cave exploring and studying the unchartered labyrinths and streams of its lower levels. They were provided with the most modern scientific instruments and equipment especially designed for their comfort, including knee and elbow pads, helmets and spiked shoes.

Who were these people? What was their reason for subjecting themselves to this ordeal which might prove an invitation to the same horrible death which overtook Floyd Collins, Lost John, and uncounted others throughout the centuries?

Their ages ranged from twenty to seventy and their occupations included a physician, a geologist, a biologist, a dancing instructor, a photographer, a housewife, a stenographer, and a student. The leader of the group was a twenty-nine-year-old electronics engineer, and they were accompanied by a reporter from the *Courier-Journal* and that same Skeets Miller, now night executive officer for the National Broadcasting Company, who speaks with modesty of his past heroism and the Pulitzer Prize which rewarded his lifesaving efforts.

Doctors examined the group to see whether its members were physically and psychologically fit for the trip. None must have claustrophobia or an anxiety neurosis since some spots in the passage were only fourteen inches wide and others a mere nine inches in depth. Pits and sheer drops, which would endanger life and limb, occurred often.

All during the past month the explorers had been in training, attempting to develop seldom-used muscles by crawling under beds and low stools. They were required to step onto a twenty-inch-high stool thirty times a minute for five minutes so that their stamina could be checked and they were given a questionnaire presenting many psychiatric posers since they would have to endure the stress of living together in the darkness through many hours of stress with the added discomfort of unusually bulky clothing and merely basic rations.

Three of the women were eliminated for one reason or another, and the final group was composed of the two remaining women and fifty-three men, many of these being volunteers who would assist the scientists, help in the communication center, and deliver the nearly two tons of material to the supply depot a mile inside the cave.

They went in on the night of February 14 and endured the torture of the first crawl-way, setting up camp on the rocking underground terrain two hundred feet below the surface. They had skirted the Bottomless Pit where the ledge was six to twelve inches wide and the only protection a thin steel cable which had been strung for them—did any of them, we wonder, know about young Courtland who had had no cable, no knee pads, for *his* Bottomless Pit?

Day by day telephone reports were made. The "moles" reported that their strangest sensation came from their inability to distinguish between night and day, their only lights being the carbide lamps which they carried.

By the end of the fourth day it was noticed that nerves were tensing. "Little men" known only to cave dwellers appeared with greater frequency and louder voices. Phantom lights shone before tired eyes.

There is a word for it. That word is "speleopsychosis."

The food was an unvarying diet of oatmeal, spaghetti, beans, raw carrots, vitamin pills. And all were flavored with sand.

Ablutions were skimpy, the two women settling for facials via cosmetic pads, and the bearded men contenting themselves with a-lick-and-a-promise from the icy underground springs, the general comment being, "I feel like something you'd find under a rock."

When the long week was up and the party returned "top level" their eyes were unable to focus in the daylight for some time, and they noted, as had every cave dweller in the past, that the smells of the good earth seemed strangely pungent. The sky was a brighter blue than they had remembered it, and the pine trees had never seemed so richly green—so beautiful to behold.

Waiting newspapermen got reports that the expedition was considered successful. Its leader believed Crystal Cave could dispute Mammoth Cave in its claim of being the largest in the world, although neither is, as yet, fully surveyed. He mentioned high waterfalls and a subterranean river which they had heard but been unable to reach, a whole new cave system within the labyrinthine paradise, the possibility of a new antibiotic which the microbiologist planned to report to his pharmaceutical company, excellent work one of the women had done in tagging and studying bats. . . .

Perhaps they'd all like to go back in the cave for another week, one of the newsmen suggested. The spelunkers looked doubtful as they headed for hot baths, soft beds, and the various other trappings of modern civilization.

CHAPTER 17

Kentucky Tour

Shrines and Shadows

On KENTUCKY AUTOMOBILE license plates for the last several years has appeared the peremptory order: "Tour Kentucky." Apparently a good many travelers take it to heart, for the state's tourist business has been tremendous since the opening of her "great lakes."

But aside from them, and from Mammoth Cave, the Derby, and the stock farms, there are quite a number of attractions of widely varying appeal. The moving memorial to Lincoln at Hodgenville, the Audubon Shrine, Levi Jackson Wilderness Road State Park with its remarkable collection of ancient millstones, and the replica of the first Kentucky stockade at Harrodsburg—a place that takes the imagination and holds it spellbound—and the Mountain Laurel Festival (if it's springtime, naturally) are worth the trouble to see.

Then there are Natural Bridge and Pine Mountain, General Butler Park, and Pennyrile Forest State Park, Jefferson Davis's birthplace and monument, Cumberland Falls Park, and Cumberland Gap.

Visits may be paid to the Dr. Thomas Walker Memorial, Old Mulkey Meeting House, Danville's "Constitution Square,"

Perryville Battlefield, Bernheim Forest, and many another beauty spot.

And the ghost village of Shakertown, near Harrodsburg, should not be overlooked for it is as quaint and picturesque a spot as one could find anywhere. The remains of this sect (a scant half dozen) moved to another community and sold their holdings in 1922. The settlement was started in 1860 and, though marriage was taboo and the sexes were strictly separated, it flourished for a number of years and the Brethren erected a depot and hotel as well as the sturdy "family buildings." The hotel, or Tavern as it was called, is a handsome structure with white-columned porticoes and an upper porch which, in olden times, was lined with rocking chairs for the comfort of gaily dressed visitors whose bright attire was a contrast to the drab simplicity of the clothes worn by the Shakers themselves.

An elderly Negro handyman remembers former residents well, and speaks of their tireless industry, quiet ways, and absolute honesty. He is quoted as saying that even at a funeral the bad as well as the good characteristics of a man were reported. When a certain blacksmith was being buried many people praised him, but one man, feeling the call of duty, rose to his feet and said, "He never *could* shoe a horse right—burned more iron than he used. He wasn't a thrifty man, to my thinking!"

There are a number of historic cemeteries in Kentucky, and many a lonely little family burying ground, set off by a rock fence in the corner of a corn field, overgrown in briers and honeysuckle.

Kentuckians today are occasionally requested to move some ancestors' bones as the new turnpike's bulldozers disturb their slumbers. One such case recently came on a somewhat macabre situation. Far below the depth at which a particular ancestor was presumably resting, the spades of the diggers struck metal, finally uncovering a heavy metal casket, unquestionably one of the first of its kind ever buried here. A glass plate had been set in the top of it, and through it could be clearly discerned the perfectly preserved face of the dead man. After one hundred and fifty years, the coffin, buried deep in the cold, cold ground, had not returned this particular body to dust but had kept it as in the midst of life.

A ghostly dwelling a tourist might like to see is White Hall, near Foxtown, home of Cassius Marcellus Clay, "Lion of White Hall," a man who for almost a century "lived a life of incredible color and conflict," most of it spent in this house, deserted now for some fifty years except for the casual occupancy of tenant families.

A legendary snake is supposed to live in the cellar. When it gets thirsty for Kentucky River water it is supposed to wend its way to that several-miles-distant stream. The old story goes that "Cash" Clay brought it home from Russia, after he had served under Abraham Lincoln's appointment as minister there for six years. The whisper of treasure there has caused much prying through spider webs and mountains of tobacco cloth and broken furniture that clutter the place. Chickens peck at the feed sacks that shroud the rosewood piano, but the classic columns in the ballroom still preserve their elegance, as does the graceful stairway.

Clay's blood-and-thunder *Memoirs*, published in 1886, caused a sensation, but copies of the book are rare; his family bought up as many as they could lay hands on, and burned them because of their frankness. Always a figure of controversy, he was one of the most determined champions of anti-slavery in the nation. His newspaper, *The True American*, which he published practically singlehanded in Lexington before the Civil War, caused such furore that the building was attacked and the presses dismantled by his opponents. For a long time he held out against repeated siege by lining the doors of the place with sheet iron and keeping a supply of Mexican lances, guns, and bowie knives with which to defend it. A violent man, ready to defend the slightest derogatory remark, he was very adept and frequently used his weapons, both before and after the dramatic career of *The True American*.

At eighty-four, long-since divorced from his strong-willed wife, "Cash" married a fifteen-year-old tenant girl. Not surprisingly, this venture too was unsuccessful, and he spent his last years in this ghostly decaying house alone, except for the colonies of bats living comfortably behind the shutters against the house wall by day and flitting through the broken windows into and out of the house at night.

In contrast to desolate White Hall is Liberty Hall built in Frankfort in 1796 by the Honorable John Brown, aide to Lafayette in the Revolutionary War, later Kentucky's first senator, an intimate of Jefferson, Madison, and Monroe. A beautiful Georgian house, its gardens terraced to the river, it is an attractive museum containing many original furnishings, including Gilbert Stuart and Matthew Jouett family portraits.

The Orlando Brown (son of John Brown) House nearby is a similar shrine. Houses all over Kentucky abound in family portraits—many of them very fine ones. (See Edna Talbott Whitley's recent *Kentucky Ante-Bellum Portraiture*.) Among the popular landscapes of yore often found on Kentucky walls are Carl Brenner's, or Harvey Joiner's "Beeches," usually shadow-boxed. Paul Sawyer's water colors are perennial, too, the old "Covered Bridge at Frankfort" being a favorite. Time was when the law required that covered bridges be erected at stipulated intervals for the protection of travelers in bad weather. The last one has long since vanished, the largest and handsomest of them all having been the historic Frankfort span.

Anybody touring Kentucky will delight in the approach to this snug valley town, divided by the curving Kentucky River, walled by knobs with their great gray faces of rock. A tourist first sees the town from the top of one of its encircling hills— the "new" Capitol, the quaint and charming old Statehouse, the scenic cemetery on its high cliff plateau, the town's suburbs scattered like Swiss chalet-villages here and there on the hillsides, and below in the leafy valley the steeples, bridges, and chimneys new and old.

Bringing railroads into the capital city was a great problem, the river and its tributary Benson Creek being the only level approaches. The tunnel cutting under the Town Hill and the cemetery was one of the first successful engineering projects of comparable size in the state.

The Old Capitol Hotel, burned years ago and replaced, was the hostelry for uncounted notables, witnessed several hot-blooded murders, and entertained many a brilliant Assembly Ball and private party. Its elaborate ballroom had a unique feature—a set of huge iron springs like bedsprings was set under the floor, so that dancers actually felt as if they were treading on air when it gave to the rhythm, and nobody could possibly get tired.

Up the hill from the hotel is the old state arsenal, its big cannon fired only to celebrate Democratic presidents' elections since Civil War days, so they say.

Will S. Hays (William Shakespeare Hays), a newspaperman, weatherman, steamboat captain, and song writer, composed (or adapted from an old Scottish air) the song "Dixie," set the words to it, and sold it to the Oliver Ditson Company for about $1,500. Though Mr. Emmett also claimed the authorship of the song, Kentuckians hold that Ditson's purchase of the expensive copyright proves Mr. Hays's rightful ownership as its writer. Two million copies of Hays's "Molly Darling" made him Kentucky's leading song writer.

Many of the Christy Minstrel songs, often ghostwritten by Stephen Foster, are among museum songs in Kentucky today. Again the searchers for famous Kentucky firsts do well to make Frankfort the scene of their treasure hunts.

The lovely old Statehouse is now the Historical Society, with as fine a historical library and museum as can be found, preserving traditional mementoes. There are stories in every nook and cranny, old flags, old manuscripts, old records galore, costumes, weapons, portraits, furniture.

Kentucky culture has been a traditional one for so many years that a tourist is rarely asked—as one is in newer communities—"How do you like Kentucky?" Right or wrong the answer is taken for granted, or perhaps not even thought about.

Kentuckians are well accustomed to criticism, and delight in criticizing each other and occasionally themselves. But there is a complacency that comes with age to any region, and it is noticeable here. Nothing another Kentuckian does amazes the others very much, either.

Much attention was given in the general press when Grandma Sprouse up near Louisa married her Delbert when she was eighty and he nineteen. . . . Now that they have celebrated their tenth anniversary—at ninety and twenty-nine— their friends say it's simply an example of the old belief that "opposites attract."

Back to Nature

A summer tourist in the hills can find a good deal of local color. Exchange a "Howdy!" with a passing lad carrying a mysterious-looking short thick pole, and you may be asked to go "huckleberrying."

The pole he carries is called a "bark" and is a container for the delicious purplish berries. These barks can be made in a jiffy, but they are said to bring luck to the gatherer if they are fashioned in the dark of the moon.

A bark is made of a poplar trunk about eight inches thick. Ring it with a hatchet, you are told, about a foot above the ground. Another ring must be cut about four feet above the first. A lengthwise slash from ring to ring is then cut, and the bark peels off easily in one big stovepipe-shaped piece. Pierce this with holes along each edge and lace it with strips of bark or a few feet of pocket string. Run a few sticks crisscross to stop up the opening at the bottom and stop the leaks with pawpaw leaves, though other varieties will do. The same sort of leaf and swig stopper can be made for the top when the tube is "lippin'" full of berries.

The berries actually keep better in these bark containers. We realize that this colorful method of packaging is far behind the times, and we admit that a lot of huckleberrying is done in buckets, but this bark method is still actually and fairly frequently done.

There is more preparation than merely preparing your bark, dear tourist, before you go after the berries seriously.

The next step in the preparation for this jaunt is to gird yourself against snakebite by wrapping friction tape around your pants legs and ankles to meet your shoes. You must also provide yourself with a handful of coarse salt and a bottle of kerosene—just in case. (This remedy, you will be glad to know, is suggested for external, rather than internal use, and it works for "chiggers" as well as snakes.)

The tramping and climbing may be rough, sweetest fruit always growing in distant pastures, but the reward will be worth the effort, for in the shadow of some upland pine tree you'll be able to pick a gallon without stirring from the spot. The trick is to hang a small bucket on a stout leather belt and use both hands, feeding them into your bark from time to time.

A further trick is to make the berries into a deep-dish pie and down it with plenty of golden-rich country milk!

Next day, if you're still in the mood for rural entertainment, you might go "noodling." Noodling is the sport of catching snapping turtles barehanded.

The proper technique is to creep along the creek bed on hands and knees, groping under ledges for your prey. When you find it you yank it out and stuff it in a burlap sack in anticipation of the feast-to-come. Some noodlers use hooked rods, but the adepts scorn such refinements, preferring the implements that were made before forks.

Lawrenceburg, in Anderson County, specializes in the sport, and every May and June its ponds and shallow creeks attest the skill of local noodlers. Three- and four-pounders are considered the best eating, although sometimes the snappers grow more than twice that large, and there are stories of ancient ones attaining a size greater than that of a full-sized galvanized washtub.

Enthusiasts will tell you that there are five different flavors of meat in the hard-shell turtle—"chicken, fish, pork, beef, and —well, turtle"—and that their own particular recipes are unique in tastiness.

In your slow swing around the state, you may see fishermen "jigging" along the banks of creeks. This is done with a long pole and a short line equipped with some jingling spinners and a worm for bait. Jiggled or jigged in the crevasses along a rocky bank, the spinners attract and the worm is snapped up by lunkers along the shore.

The uninhibited country fisherman will stick his hand under

any submerged rock, with the hope of taking out a big fish. He may get a snake, but it's all in the day's play. . . .

Little Lost Pikes

We would like to recommend seriously a turnoff for the tourist who has a little extra time to leave the big highways. Any of the little gray pikes held over from time gone by will do, and will give you one or more of Kentucky's subtlest vintage flavors.

Your trip may be a wild one. Your pike may zigzag along river cliffs, dip into ravines where rabbits and possums and other little animals scoot from your wheels in Disneyland profusion. These little pikes are narrow and twisting—sometimes climbing a hill to see what's on the other side, and coming back on the same side.

It may lead through the gentlest, richest farmlands in the world, our little pike, to show you masses of larkspur growing in thick wheat stubble, day lilies and primroses and Queen Anne's lace crowding the roadside, with rye and oats and alfalfa and clover and corn, and tobacco and all, in the fertile fields beyond the fences.

It may cross and recross a little stream, interrupt colonies of indigo buntings nesting in the huge brier or elder bushes on either side of the road. It will have the most wonderful butterflies, as blue as the chickory "daisies" all along the way. It will have hundreds of tiny gold finches and tons and tons of trumpet vine where hummingbirds feast constantly all summer. It will have duckberry vines (bittersweet) and tall velvety false tobacco (mullein) and golden rod and Bouncing Bet.

It sharpens the senses to take to the byways. The unimproved houses are so remote and comfortably resigned-looking. One can't hurry, has no wish to. There is no traffic problem, and all the sights and sounds and smells of sweet deep country are yours. You can stop to try to identify unusual birds or flowers, wade for a few moments in a crystal creek with a bed of such even limestone slabs that they must have been put there, one feels, by hand.

It's rather nice to pass the time of day (with no argument about it!) with an occasional farmer working near the pike, or watch a distant thrasher puffing, stop to read the brave field-stone markers in a fenced-off burying ground, eat a handful of warm dusty blackberries, drink a swallow of icy spring water, or just listen to the bees and smell the hay.

A dirt farmer working his land—and indeed the very land itself—exudes unhurried accomplishment, a sense of self-sufficiency, of tasks always being done and never quite finished, an accepted and comfortable loneliness, a particular peace. The cushiony roots of unkempt deep-country grass seem tougher, more resilient than those of smooth city lawns. One feels that everything lasts longer, that sounds are more distinct, the sun warmer, the shade cooler, the breeze sweeter, the quiet quieter.

Of course if one lingers till dusk, and then seeks directions to the main highway, the thundering herd thereon and the sunset of neon pinks and purples, there may be a moment or so of bewilderment.

One old Kentucky porch-sitter we asked for directions told us rather gruffly to get back the way we came. Since his cabin was the only one around, we tried again to pry out some information, the way we'd come being hazy in our minds.

"Where does this road go?" we asked.

"Lot o' places."

"Do you know where the nearest road marker is?"

He didn't. He didn't know where the nearest town was, he

insisted, or the bridge we kept describing, or that church at a crossroads somewhere. "He doesn't know much, does he?" somebody in our exploring party murmured. He evidently heard it, for his reply was sharp and mischievous.

"Mebbe not. But I ain't lost!"

Index

CLARK McMEEKIN

Dorothy Park Clark   *Isabel McLennan McMeekin*

For almost twenty years—"without fussin', feudin', or fightin'"—Clark McMeekin has been an amicable and successful writing partnership, establishing something of a record, not only for Kentucky but also for the literary world.

Mrs. McMeekin has lived all of her life in Louisville, where her mother's ancestors were among the early settlers. Her husband, Samuel H. McMeekin, was an executive of Churchill Downs until his retirement in 1956.

Mrs. Clark, who was brought up in Lexington and Frankfort, has lived in Louisville for some thirty years. Her husband, Edward R. Clark, is secretary of the Brown Wood-Preserving Company and the Brown Hotels.

The Clark McMeekin historical novels began with SHOW ME A LAND, and the latest is THE OCTOBER FOX (1956). In between were RECKON WITH THE RIVER, WELCOME SOLDIER, BLACK MOON, RED RASKALL, GAUDY'S LADIES, CITY OF THE FLAGS, ROOM AT THE INN, and TYRONE OF KENTUCKY.

Legendary tales of other generations, courthouse records, family letters, Kentucky politics, the tragedies of families divided by Civil War, Kentucky background materials of whatever period have always been engrossing subjects to both halves of the Clark McMeekin partnership, and in OLD KENTUCKY COUNTRY the most entertaining and effective use has been made of these grass roots of history.

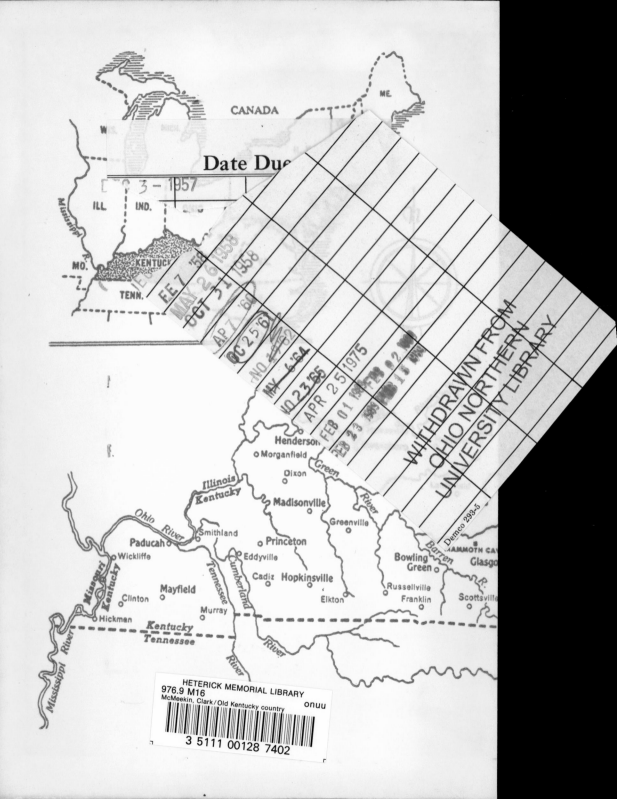

CANADA

ME.

WIS.   MICH.

ILL.   IND.   OHIO

MO.

KENTUCKY

TENN.

Mississippi R.

Henderson
Morganfield
Dixon
Green River
Illinois
Kentucky
Madisonville
Greenville
Ohio   River
Smithland
Paducah
Wickliffe
Eddyville
Princeton
Bowling
Green
Barren R.
Glasgow
MAMMOTH CAVE
Tennessee
Cumberland
Cadiz   Hopkinsville
Russellville
Franklin
Scottsville
Mayfield
Clinton
Elkton
Murray
Missouri
Kentucky
Hickman
Kentucky
Tennessee
River
River